WWII AMERICAN WAR EAGLES 1937-1942

America's ARSENAL of DEMOCRACY - Vol. 1

12656

Warren M. Bodie

ALL ORIGINAL *KODACHROME* COLOR

Dedication

By the time this book first appears on the shelves of bookstores and in private domiciles, I will have mourned the passing of my wife of 45 years, Catherine Larson Bodie for almost exactly a dozen years. The impact she had on my life, as I look back, was nothing but astonishing. I cannot imagine loving any other person with the enduring intensity with which I loved her. And it has not diminished a bit. Absence does make the heart grow fonder, if that is possible. Therefore, I dedicate this book to her memory. I know she will not mind sharing the dedication with one man with whom we bonded so well when he lived. That person is B/Gen. Benjamin Kelsey, USAAF, Retired (now deceased). I have not met a person who served under or with Ben who did not have great affection for him. If there were any, they just did not understand his brilliance and his desire to do a marvelous job without making any enemies. Therefore, as one of the best friends a man can have, he deserves this dedication of one of my best efforts. He was an inspirational man

Published in the United States of America by:
Widewing Publications
Created, owned and operated solely by:
Warren M. Bodie, Author-Publisher
81 Sneaking Creek Lane
Hayesville, NC 28904

Copyright © **Widewing Publications** 2001
ISBN 0-9629359-4-8

Book design & Color Artwork by Bob Boyd, Roswell, GA.

Printed in China by Pettit Enterprises, Afton, MN.

Widewing Publications holds International distribution rights.
MBI Publishing Co., parent of Motorbooks International (MBI/Zenith Books), Osceola, WI, holds North American distribution rights to the trade.

Frontispiece: Although this corpulent, pugnacious little Grumman F2F-1 naval shipboard fighter was only about six years of age in 1940-41, it had become incredibly obsolete as a combat-worthy machine. It wore the markings of a marvelous age in U.S. Navy history, colorful beyond comprehension for its deadly role as a fighter. As of 2001, it is the only color photograph of an authentic and authentically marked F2F-1 ever encountered from any source to date. As war raged in Europe, Africa and Asia, several of these fascinating machines were assigned to fighter and dive-bombing training at NAS Miami, Florida. USN cadet and amateur photographer Edward W. Simpson, Jr. encountered this spotless F2F-1 in the clear, recording it on Kodachrome for all of us to enjoy in later life.

Page 2: It would be wonderful to say that the Vought-Sikorsky SB2U-3 and nearly identical SB2U-2 scout-bombers ordered by the USN and by France in the 1930s decade had spectacular war records. Unfortunately, they met mid-1930s specifications issued by BuAer in the depth of the Great Depression, and those were not adequately advanced to provide a weapon of war that could cope with aircraft from an aggressive and determined enemy. *USMC via R. Starinchak*

Title Page: Boeing Airplane Company's brand new, just in time B-17E Flying Fortresses came along at the right time despite governmental intransigence concerning prices at the worst possible time. Fortunately, more intelligent people managed to settle the problems without forcing Boeing into bankruptcy. *Boeing*

Page 5: A stack of Stearman N2S navy trainer biplanes, almost the last of an aging breed, flies in a neat echelon formation. *USN/R. Starinchak*

Table of Contents

Acknowledgements

In some ways, collectors of World War II aviation, military and naval color photographs (specifically Kodachrome I transparencies and slides) are akin to being archeologists, or at least brothers under the skin. It was only about a decade before World War II erupted in Europe that Technicolor movie films came into being, and it was nearly another decade before Kodachrome color film for still pictures came into regular use on a small scale. Newspaper photographers only believed in large format photographs (4x5 in. primarily) in black and white. Miniature (35-mm) cameras did not impress those photographers as being viable news cameras at all. But the timing was right for E.K.'s Kodachrome film and, concurrently, the Germans were producing about the best 35-mm cameras in the world. By 1937, Americans seemed to go crazy over miniature cameras and the small format pictures were just about ideal for many. Best of all, you could take 36 exposures without changing film. As Fred Bamberger has told us in the Foreword, matching certain German cameras with Kodachrome I film gave some outstanding results. Unfortunately for the Germans, their own Agfa color films were far inferior in color stability and they tended to be grainy. Ansco color film became available in America, and processing was less expensive than the EK product. How could anyone know that color stability was not to be the forte of Ansco color film? By the turn of this century, virtually all Ansco color had disappeared – gone with the wind. Agfa color film could only be processed in Germany, and it was expensive. Also, it was far outclassed by Kodachrome. In Japan, color film was essentially unknown.

What, then, could we expect to find proliferating throughout America about six decades past World War II events? Not much, so digging for them in remote places is much like archeology. Many good commercially generated 4x5 transparencies were poorly archived, and a large percentage of them became badly stained. The U.S. Navy photographers evidently were supplied with far less Kodachrome film than Ansco film to shoot. Eventually about 90 to 100 percent of Ansco films lost their colors. Nearly forgotten in files, this problem was late in being detected. Therefore, the Navy lost thousands of color images. Evidently, the Army Ground Forces and the AAF did relatively little to protect their color film images, so the supply of official color pictures involving equipment and actions in war are rarely seen. If Norton AFB has been closed down, where did their possible collection of color go? At one time in the past, EK claimed that they knew of very little color film being exposed in WWII days by private parties. Just a few amateur photographers this author has encountered have proven that to be an incorrect premise. Obviously E.K. had no real records of how much came from that source for development. In the meantime, many WWII participants have passed away. Yet, we suspect that at least some of them took unauthorized color photographs during the war. Most certainly thousands of black & white exposures were made and processed in spite of censors. The question then arises: What has become of long ignored processed color films taken by individuals during that war? Much of it must still remain, even perhaps in dust covered slide projectors or yellow slide boxes. It all constitutes valuable history, but how can it rise, like cream, to the surface and reach those of us who can do something important with the material? Probably only by word of mouth. But we must keep on searching.

Another problem exists. Amateur photographers and even professionals like Rudy Arnold, Hans Groenhoff and perhaps Edward Steichen did almost nothing to protect those precious images. Color photos by Eric Miller have been traced to a relative, but that young person has no real interest in complying with Eric's wishes. And the years tick away. (I had done many favors for Eric and he said he wanted to let me access them, but he passed away within days.) Then there is the problem of cellophane envelopes used for cut film storage. It proved to be a bad product for storing color film. Add minor moisture and heat, and the images are seriously damaged. Acid fingerprints, fungus, handling scratches and what-have-you ruined many images. Sometimes, expensive restoration can save them. Animal fats used in the making of Kodachrome film emulsion attract microscopic vermin that eat the color material.

Just one example of the great harm that was done after WWII became history occurred at the Naval Photographic Center (NPC) at Anacostia, DC. For years there was essentially no interest in the material. Finally, one man was assigned to the task of correctly identifying times, places, subjects and film condition. Evidently, out of a total of approximately 6,000 color images, fewer than 1,000 had survived the ravages of time. Few, if any, Ansco color images had survived. Most likely literally hundreds of exposures had been loaned, purloined, discarded unintentionally, never to be returned to file. It was not unusual for images to be damaged beyond repair in attempts to rewash or somehow correct relatively minor flaws. Often a disinterested commander would order files to be purged because they had been ignored for years.

After the Civil War, hundreds of Mathew Brady's irreplaceable glass plate exposures were unintentionally destroyed because their value was not understood. The number is unknown. Aircraft companies (Douglas El Segundo Division being one) have chosen to send thousand of photographs to a dump – refusing even to give them to interested collectors or agencies. In the 1950s, Wright Field authorities destroyed nearly 25,000 films, mostly 8x10 negatives, because they were in wooden cabinets and were exuding noxious odors. They were a potential fire hazard, but officials would not even donate the material to private organizations or collectors. (One commander there, early in WWII, had many historical airplanes burned. They had been removed from buildings to obtain needed space.)

Even Col. Fred Bamberger – author of the Foreword for this book – who was one of the most prolific of all early color photographers, did nothing with the excellent color pictures he took with his own color camera during the war. His longtime associates (Harold Martin and James Hawkins) from prewar years did not follow Fred's lead and use color film until the war was virtually history. There was almost no market for color photography until well after the war ended. A current 2001 search for any color film exposed by Otto Menge or his staff at Consolidated Aircraft has only served to convince us that virtually no desire for color images existed in World War II. If the great San Francisco commercial photographer Clyde Sunderlund made any color exposures of aircraft or ships, they have yet to be found. Opportunity existed when he photographed the Pan American Airways Martin China Clipper and Sikorsky S-42 clippers over the incomplete Golden Gate Bridge in the late 1930s, but none are known to exist. The marvelous pre-war British magazines, *FLIGHT* and *AEROPLANE* evidently did not even attempt color ads. Therefore, they did not seek any color photographs.

No color photographs connected with WWII were ever known to exist in France, Japan or Russia. It is unlikely they had film, and Kodachrome film development was very restrictive. In spite of thousands of opportunities for pictures, we have seen none. Some intensive searches in England reveal (so far) that evidently few WWII Kodachromes were exposed by the Royal Navy or Royal Air Force in the British Empire. Therefore, the mighty Royal Navy ship photo coverage in color is next to nil. That is a devastating lost opportunity. From 1937 through 1939, at the very least, there was tremendous opportunity to photograph at least every important type of naval ship in the Royal Navy and the United States Navy in color…but it never happened and was probably not even considered.

It is with pleasure that I honor and commend the diligent collectors of Kodachrome images, and especially the few persons who even photographed airplanes in color between 1937 and 1946. Such images are essentially priceless when they can be reproduced in a book such as this. Fred Bamberger is no longer with us, but his life will be perpetuated in the publication of his many color images.

Collectors to whom I am deeply indebted include Richard Starinchak, Robert D. Archer, Edward Boss, Jr., Walter Boyne, Warren Thompson, Jr., Robert Astrella, Gerald Balzer, Peter M. Bowers, Robert Dorr, Wesley Henry at the Air Force Museum, Gerry Markgraf, Roger Seybel and the volunteer staff at Northrop-Grumman History Center, Fred Roos, James Sullivan and last but far from least, Edward W. Simpson, Jr. for his great original color photo work under anything but good circumstances.

Of course the men at the Naval History Center and Naval History Foundation have been of great assistance, and their most important contributions are yet to be seen in additional volumes of this title. The very fact that this list is not lengthy reveals how few real color-film "archeologists" really exist or have shown their flags.

It is no wonder that the special USAAF photographic officer, General George Goddard, was so complimentary at his meeting with Col. Fred Bamberger after the war.

Edward W. Simpson's photography was certainly on a par with the real professionals of the pre-WWII days, Rudy Arnold and Hans Groenhoff. Commander Simpson is evidently the only person who saw the importance of recording 1930s airplanes in color. Otherwise we would never have seen such wonderful aircraft as the Grumman F2F-1 and Consolidated P2Y-2 in gorgeous color. His combat pictures will appear in the other volumes of this trilogy for he was Air Group Commander aboard the aircraft carrier U.S.S. *Chenango* (CV-28) in the Pacific Theater of Operations. He flew Wildcats and Hellcats in combat.

Without the artistic expertise of Bob Boyd, not to mention his knowledge of aircraft and naval ships, this book and its future brothers would have been infinitely more difficult to produce. In the face of great pain and pressures, he "done good."

My old Lockheed associate, G. O. Glenn, has been an anchor post for support whenever I needed it. I presume it is not commonplace to laud the major distributor of your published works, but I must say that it has been a real pleasure to have Motorbooks International (MBI) in my court. Brad Siqueiros and his wonderful team in Contracts have been of infinite assistance for a decade now. They have been a delight to work with, and of tremendous help to my progress. A snappy salute to all of you from this old codger. *Warren M. Bodie, Author-Publisher*

Introduction

"Peace In Our Time!" "The War to End All Wars." "America Must Avoid All Foreign Entanglements."

So said all who believed that the United States of America was well isolated from foreign wars by the great Atlantic and Pacific Oceans plus a powerful navy that could use these mammoth bodies of water to our advantage. It was somewhat comparable to former President Herbert Hoover – a wealthy engineer by education and experience – insisting that the Great Depression that had settled in could be overcome by business and industry without governmental interference. Hoover evidently learned his politics from former President Calvin Coolidge who had a "hands off" style. It was isolation from reality; "Don't bother me with facts. My mind is made up," sort of thinking.

Some of the old-style presidents had never learned a thing from history. A very well intentioned past president, Woodrow Wilson, seemed to believe that things could be worked out by committee, and that all mankind is really good. None of these former presidents seemed to have any real connection with reality, any more than British Prime Minister Chamberlain demonstrated.

As I recall from my far distant youth, at almost any given time in the 1920s and 1930s, there were small and medium-sized wars being fought on this planet almost any day somewhere in the world. Mankind is known for his inability to avoid war. Here are just a few reminders. Japan began its conquest of China in 1931 with the seizure of the Manchurian city of Mukden. The League of Nations, formed after the end of hostilities in Continental Europe on November 11, 1918, proved to be essentially powerless to intervene. Japan forged ahead with what amounted to annexation of Manchuria, soon converted to the independent state of Manchukuo by 1932. (Abolished 1945.) This was the first of four major appeasements attributable to the League.

From 1933 to 1937, Japan continued warlike actions against China's sovereignty in five provinces north of the Yellow River. In the meantime, Chinese Communists and Nationalists forged ahead with prolonging their civil war almost until they joined forces to fight the Japanese when they struck again at the heartland of China in June 1937.

Have you ever heard of the Chako war? Well, that one raged on in South America between Paraguay and Bolivia from 1932 to 1936. Evidently the League didn't figure this war, or series of wars, were worthy of intervention or appeasement.

Ethiopia was next on the list of major appeasements. The League let boastful, swaggering Benito Mussolini attack and decimate untrained, poorly armed defenders of a small, nearly wasteland country by land and air. It was tanks and artillery against antique rifles…even spears in 1935. Almost unnoticed, this was against a backdrop of Britain and France dealing under the table to let the Ethiopians be subjugated.

Next on the list of League failures, and our national fashion of learning nothing from close observation, was the blatant arming of totalitarian Generalissimo Franco and the use of Spain as a combat training ground. It was 1936, only three years after Adolf Hitler grabbed ruling power over an inflation-plagued, depression-ridden Germany. Communist Russia retaliated – with somewhat less effect – by sending arms to the Loyalists. America, certainly a major power, did less than nothing as the League of Nations began to crumble.

This country was focused on the Depression, dust storms and isolationism, probably feeling more threatened by Communism than Nazism. Sadly, Col. Charles Lindbergh – perhaps with his thinking despoiled by the kidnapping and murder of his infant son – vented his spleen by his strong support of the America First party. Lindbergh had been "treated" to a close-up view of Nazi Germany's military strengthening and it evidently inspired him to rail against this country's involvement in foreign affairs. But aviation writers Cy Caldwell, on staff at Aero Digest magazine, and Major Al Williams as aviation spokesman for Gulf Oil Company were every bit as much aware of Nazi rearmament chose to editorialize about the need to bring the USA's defenses up to a level representative of a great power. The America First supporters, peppered with members of the German-American Bund, stupidly believed that turning the other cheek to aggressors would serve to keep them from aggression against America. Such thinking has never worked anywhere, and it never will.

Basically, good people are peace loving, but the aggressive, angry, power-hungry minority is easily duped into hating those with great assets. Their hatred eats at them until – like Hitler – it feeds upon itself. The "haves" will always be targets for the "have not" people of the world who will contrive to take those assets they could not earn or inherit. It is part of the character of mankind, and evidently nothing is likely to change that. For example, ten Latin American countries were swept by revolution during the 1930s decade.

That decade of troubled times was not selective in targeting any nation. America should have continued to prosper but its leadership failed the nation. However, no single thing was responsible for the fall from grace. World trade fell by 70 percent! Governments fell like tenpins. France turned to Socialism, setting the scene for the fall of another French Republic soon after the fall of the German Republic. If anyone believes that Hitler's, Mussolini's and François only existed outside of North America, they too are delusional. Demagogues preyed on human weakness in America too. Governor Huey "Kingfish" Long, Gerald L. K. Smith and Michigan's Father Coughlin made the most of hate, fear, intolerance and bitterness about the state of affairs afflicting the "have not" people in the same ways that Lenin, Stalin, Hitler and Mussolini did in the same decade. Similar militaristic leaderships in Japan and Chinese warlords on the mainland drew less attention on the part of Americans more submerged in their local problems. All of this, of course, set the table for a devastating world war. As anyone knows, undercurrents are more to be feared than currents. In such an environment, isolationism grew to the detriment of strength. We failed ourselves in not maintaining armed forces commensurate with our world power status.

Finally, it all came to smiling, hat-in-hand Prime Minister Neville Chamberlain and Premier Edouard Daladier (1939-40) traveling to Munich, Germany, with some flaccid hope of persuading Adolf Hitler – who must have ultimately collapsed from hysterical laughter – to "please refrain from further expansionism" or at least something close to such phraseology.

Now the stage was set for creation of the Arsenal of Democracy in America, although few if any even had a clue. In embracing Socialism, France had inadvertently ruined its armaments industry, especially in the aeronautical structure. Great Britain's pompous, Etonian-styled statesman deluded the populace with myths about German intentions, forgetting that the path to Hell is paved with good intentions. Too late the French leaders tried to create a defense system, but it was anchored in more ways than one by the Maginot Line. Again, the French had failed to understand the German militaristic mind. The British were living on hope; the French were in panic when they turned to America with its wealth of idle production capacity. Not many years prior to 1939, France's air power was considered absolute tops in the world. Now it had shriveled to but a shadow of its former self. Its first-line aircraft were terribly obsolete – even by American standards based on the ideas that thousands of miles of ocean waters protected us (a fluid form of the Maginot Line), reinforced by a World War I naval force weakened further by the Washington Naval Treaty agreement. (Humans never seem to learn that the "bad guys" will never honor any agreements on paper or by a handshake. They only respect strength.)

Few people realize that it was France that saved our own aircraft and engine industry from the verge of bankruptcy in the late Thirties. Those industrial entities were being forced to the brink of starvation by their own legislators. French gold came to the rescue of companies such as Pratt & Whitney and probably Curtiss. It was the Swedes, not Americans, who staved off the wolves of bankruptcy at Seversky Aircraft – again aiding P&W Division of United Aircraft Corporation in the process. And British gold, strangely preceded by cash from Japan (for Model 14 Super Electra commercial aircraft), kept tiny Lockheed Aircraft in Burbank afloat with massive orders for a militarized version of that same type called the Hudson.

And then it was an ordinary spring day in May 1940. What presidential incumbent since the days of Teddy Roosevelt would have had the perspicacity and fortitude shown on the 16th day of that month to propose that Congress authorize the expansion of aircraft production to 50,000 airplanes a year? Certainly it could only have been (since the beginning of the century) another man with the Roosevelt name. Like the FDR style or hate it, he was *the* one president of all who would have made such an astounding commitment and request. It may have been just another day, but its implications shook America to its foundations. And it was the right thing to do.

Actually, regardless of Admiral Yamamoto's statement to the effect that Japan's attack on Pearl Harbor and the Philippines had awakened a "sleeping giant," it was our president who had blown the bugle on May 16, 1940. Not only for the aircraft industry, but also for naval shipbuilding, tank and military truck production, and a plethora of other military and naval weaponry.

Few seem aware that Roosevelt (not Teddy) had managed to gain the approval of Congress to authorize construction of the first new battleships by FY1940 – no fewer than SEVENTEEN of them – since THREE battleships of the Class of 1916 were authorized *during* World War I! Included in that astonishing group of seventeen were six in the North Carolina Class of 1937-38, six in the Iowa Class of 1939-40 and five of the Montana Class of 1940. A startling fact is buried in that revelation about Roosevelt's amazing ability to do something no other president since 1916 had been able to do. It should be pointed out that the five Montana Class battleships ordered in 1940 – more than a year prior to the Pearl Harbor attack – were never completed despite the most intensive efforts to complete them. Not one of the five enormous 58,000-ton Montana Class juggernauts was ever completed. They were the length of a football field and each carried a dozen 16-inch guns. All were canceled in 1943, very close to three years after they were ordered on 9 Sept. 1940. Why? By that time, it was pretty clear to our planners that the tide was definitely in our favor, the Japanese had lost at least a few first-line battleships in combat while we had lost none. In fact the IJN had lost nine battleships by the time the surrender documents were signed aboard the USS *Missouri* (BB63) in August 1945.

Thanks to our pre-war Two-Ocean Fleet building program initiated well before the Pearl Harbor episode, the U.S. Navy had an amazing twenty-three battleships in full service in the summer of 1945 as Japan was being softened up for invasion. That number included six fully rebuilt and modernized ships that had been severely damaged in the December 7, 1941, attack. Since naval warfare had – because of the changing complexion of sea warfare – swung from the WWI-type of dreadnaught command of the seas to aircraft carrier warfare, there was no real need for new 58,000-ton super battleships. Even the USS *Illinois* (BB65), an Iowa Class battleship was cancelled (after V-J Day) because the keel had not even been laid until 15 January 1945. During the hostilities, no fewer than seventeen fast Essex Class aircraft carriers (CVs) joined the fleet plus nine light Independence Class CVLs. It is important to know that eleven of the Essex Class CVs and eight of nine Independence Class CVLs had been ordered in 1940.[1]

Just where would we have been if the standing president of the United States had not had the vision to order a dozen other 35,000 and 45,000-ton battlewagons in the midst of depression followed by a recession? In fact five of those 58,000-ton Montana Class of 1940 monsters were ordered in September 1940. With a large portion of our old WWI battleships sitting on the bottom of Pearl Harbor, or at least severely damaged, had it not been for our Arsenal of Democracy ability to repair and rebuild those ships, we might well have been in far worse shape to fight the Japanese. The Two-Ocean Fleet construction ordered in the 1930s and 1940 were prime elements in our ability to defeat the Japanese and destroy their major expansionist movements in Asia.

[1] Five of the CVL hulls had been laid down as light cruisers, but had been reordered as CVLs on 18 March 1942.

Although the first Grumman F4F airplane of the type to be known eventually as the Wildcat was ordered on July 28, 1936, on BuAer Contract 46973 as the XF4F-2, the initial production F4F-3 was not delivered until 1940. Thanks to what the Japanese learned from their purchase of the Vought V-173 airplane, design data and tooling, development of the Mitsubishi Type 0 and the Nakajima Ki.43 Hayabusa moved forward at a much greater pace. The total number of F4F airplanes built by Grumman was only 1,547, although total Wildcat production came to a grand total of 7,916, the bulk of that total flowing from the Eastern Aircraft Division of General Motors. (The strange part of that situation is that quickly converted automotive plants in the Atlantic States area built far more good FM-1, FM-2 and Martlet fighters than long-time producer Brewster Aeronautical could ever have built of any type during its existence.) This photograph shows Grumman F4F-4s on the deck of the escort carrier USS *Santee* in 1942 in the Pacific Ocean area of conflict. *USN*

Aviation in Kodachrome - The War Years
Fred Bamberger, Col. USAF (Ret.) - Pioneer

A reader might well wonder why a person in his octogenarian years, quite relaxed and living the good life, agrees to write a Foreword for a book. In all my active 83 years, I had never been approached about such a matter. It was a friend, Author-Publisher Warren Bodie who made me aware of the important part I played in aviation color photography in the 1930s and '40s when some marvelous new camera and film technologies appeared on the horizon. In the midst of the Great Depression in America and other parts of the world, Kodachrome film and a handful of new German 35mm cameras arrived with little more than a murmur.

In the late '90s, Col. Freddie Bamberger was pictured thusly at an aviation museum in Florida, a state that is also his current home. He was, by then, an octogenarian, and still handy with a camera and color film. Do you suppose they posed him in front of "Old Crow" with some underhanded intentions? No, not Fred. He is too personable. Fred has led the good life. *Via Bamberger*

Actually, that is something that should be recognized as perhaps being as important as the part Matthew Brady played in photographing Civil War scenes. World War I was obviously photographed entirely in monotones of black and white. As Warren's Widewing Publications books reveal, color in World War II was in its infancy. It was comparable to the development level of aircraft in World War I. Fortunately for me, various factors combined to propel me toward becoming one of the pioneers in the use of Kodachrome, especially in the field of aviation. It seems logical to tell at least one part of that important story.

My first real interest in aviation was directly connected to that universally great event, Charles Lindbergh's flight across the Atlantic Ocean to Paris, France, in 1927. Just that one event had raised interest in aviation to levels unseen since the end of WWI, even beyond that. But a few short years later, virtually every business in America was in a doldrums of unimaginable magnitude. My family suffered serious financial reverses, so attending college was not an immediately viable option. Dozens, perhaps hundred, of aircraft businesses had disappeared from the scene. In contrast, the aviation magazine business seemed to expand, especially the so-called pulp magazines. Concurrently, by 1932 the family finances had improved to an extent that I began to write articles for *Model Airplane News* and others. In order to support the articles with proper photographs, I began to tour the airport circuit and take pictures for that purpose. My dad had a friend who owned a nearby camera shop, allowing me to make some "good deals" as the needs arose. Two other local shutter bugs (as we were called in those days) - Harold G. Martin and James Hawkins - always teamed with me at every opportunity. Both were ultimately to become professional aviation photographers.

Almost incredibly, in a very tight job market, I had joined the Emerson Radio organization, providing a tiny but adequate income. In my spare time, I could usually be found at some local or distant airport with my friends, and we often encountered others with the same interest in aviation. Through the magazine connection, a rather loose-knit organization of aircraft photographers was formed. It was the IAAPE, International Amateur Aircraft Photo Exchange, formed in New Jersey. Before long, it became a national - even international - group, proving to be a dynamite source for contacting other airplane photo collectors everywhere. Naturally, it became a tiny stock exchange for trading negatives, prints and information. In those times there was a film size identified as 116 and also 616. The film provided a large format well suited to the shape of airplanes, e.g., 2³/₄x4¹/₂ inches, in inexpensive roll film packaging. Eastman Kodak manufactured a serixes of cameras that were available at modest prices. A few hobbyists were able to afford Zeiss Ikonta cameras from Germany, and some even used cut film cameras such as the Graflex and even Speed Graphic press cameras. They were inherently few in number in a nation suffering from business stagnation. Harold Martin and I joined the U.S. Marine Corps Reserves in 1933, primarily because that status carried with it wide access to military and naval aircraft not available to civilians. We made the most of it to record images of interesting airplanes of the era. For the first half of the decade, all of our photography was centered on use of black and white film in the now extinct 116/616 film, mostly of the orthographic type. When the owner of the camera shop allowed me to try out one of his newly arrived German 35-mm "miniature" cameras, he even permitted me to make my own selection from those on hand. I chose the Zeiss Contax and was soon exposing b&w film, generally available in 24- and 36-exposure cassettes. Within a very short time, I was taking photographs from the rear cockpit of a somewhat archaic Curtiss O2C-1 Helldiver biplane. The non-bellows, small-sized Contax was optimum for that sort of activity. Hal Martin and I operated out of NAS Floyd Bennett Field, and at times we could be seen at NAS Anacostia, immediately adjacent to the Army's Bolling Field at Washington, D.C. Those same bases, and others, provided some dramatic access to the scene with opportunities to photograph rare vintage and experimental aircraft flown in by military and naval pilots, many of who were to play key roles in a not-too-distant war. By that time I had also upgraded my basic - read that as my IAAPE - camera to a Zeiss Ikomat D that used 116-size film. The Zeiss Tessar lens produced images of high quality compared to the lenses in standardized EK Vigilant and Monitor cameras.

Kodachrome color photography was restricted to a miniscule segment of the masses until 35mm cameras - including some superb German products with color-corrected lenses - became readily available in the second half of the decade. My arrival at the doors of manhood entered into the equation about the same time in the mid-1930s. About this time, American 35mm cameras appeared on the scene and I was totally intrigued with the concept. Relatively inexpensive Argus A-2 and the better C-3 models were suitable for most amateurs in photography, but the exciting cameras were the new Leica and the Zeiss Contax cameras from Germany. Both were priced far out of my range. The outstanding LIFE magazine came aboard in that era too, but quite incredibly, even the pictorial ads were generally in black & white graphics. Speed Graphic 4x5 cameras with the1/ 1000th of a second focal plane shutters were the rage of the time for press photographers. Few of them believed that anything could improve on large format film images.

(Of course they were eventually proven wrong.)

By 1936 I discovered that my foreman's brother was the Night Editor for Acme Newspictures, a division of the New York World Telegram newspaper. I made arrangements for an introduction, gathered some samples of my photo work and went to that editor. I quickly learned that they did not need another cameraman but they really wanted somebody to work in the darkroom on the 9pm-to-6am shift. That "Lobster Shift" job paid less money than I was currently making, but I had a gut feeling that this was the way to go for the future. I took the job. It was a good decision. I would arrive home at 7 AM and sleep until noon, a schedule allowing me to attend college from 2 until 6.

In addition to working in the Acme darkroom, I was occasionally called to go on a news assignment. It was great working in this "highly charged" photojournalism atmosphere. It also gave me the opportunity to familiarize myself with the latest press equipment and lenses to enhance my own knowledge. One benefit was the opportunity for me to work with a truly early "legend" in the business, a

Fred won his wings and was commissioned a Second Lieutenant in the Air Corps Reserve in October 1941 just as the new Army Air Force was expanding at ever increasing rates. Incredibly, he was sent to the "West Point of the Air" also known as Randolph Field in Texas. Named after Capt. Wm. E. Randolph, who died in an airplane crash in 1928, the major training site for the Air Corps was dedicated on June 20-21, 1930, at San Antonio. The beautiful domed tower marked the administration building, its Spanish architecture gleaming white in the sun. Fred's new office was located in that tower, generally referred to as the "Taj Mahal." Armed with his reliable Contax 35mm camera and a supply of Kodachrome I film, he was suddenly in "hog heaven."   *Fred Bamberger*

man widely known as "WeeGee." Arthur Fellig was his real name, and he was a freelancer living in a room across the street from police headquarters in New York City. His entire operation was a pioneering venture in press coverage with his Speed Graphic camera and flashgun. He became famous in the 1930s, the Walter Winchell era of radio.

There was an opportunity for me to discuss the merits of these splendid new cameras with some of the top-rated cameramen on the staff. Without exception, they felt it was a 'toy' that could not be taken seriously. They condemned the negatives as being too small, the cameras as not well suited to news photography. Their strong opinions failed to convince me that I was wrong

Working at the news organization, I was acutely aware of world affairs because of the constant outpouring of news from the office Teletype machines. The situation in Europe was deteriorating by the day. Flying frequently in military aircraft by late 1937 really made me appreciate my status in life. Although I had not yet completed the two years of college necessary for flying cadet appointment, I decided to apply anyway. Lacking the necessary college credits, it was necessary for me to take some 18 hours of exams encompassing nine subjects. In the so-called Roosevelt Recession of that period, the application list was lengthy and the rejection rate was extremely high. By November 1937 I completed my 4-year tour in the Marine Corps Reserve and had great expectations of getting into the Army Air Corps cadet program. That meant facing numerous examining boards, surviving many physical exams and batteries of written tests.

It was anti-climatic to be accepted after a couple of years of sincere effort.

Coincidentally, several brands of 35mm color film were becoming available, but Kodak's Kodachrome seemed to offer the best results. The first roll of that film moved through my Contax camera early in 1937 at North Beach Airport, a site that later blossomed into LaGuardia Field. By the time I entered the cadet program I had gained some good experience with, and a working knowledge of, color film. Concurrently, the moment had arrived for me to enter the world of my first love, the military airplane with a totally new outlook, especially when I was airborne in the cockpit of those yellow-winged Stearman PT-17 trainers. Suffice to say, those days were memorable and passed all too quickly.

By October 13, 1940, I was commissioned as a Second Lieutenant in the Air Corps Reserve. Suddenly and unexpectedly, the world became my oyster. I was given an assignment as Post Photographic Officer at Randolph Field, San Antonio, Texas, the absolutely fabulous "West Point of the Air." (That assignment was akin to putting the fox in charge of the hen house. It is totally doubtful that any other photographic officer in the Army Air Corps would ever have been ecstatic about photographing old Air Corps and Navy airplanes, especially in color in 1940. - Ed.)

My duties were varied and many and my photo lab was located in one of the most prestigious structures in the AAF, the Randolph Field tower, more affection-

Settling in the rear seat of a North American BT-14 trainer with a camera believed to be an F-8 aerial camera (too big to be a K-20), Fred appears to be about ready to go on yet one more photo mission from the beautiful Randolph flying field. Although the base was served primarily by NAA BT-9s and BT-14s in pre-Pearl Harbor days, there was a plethora of everything from Paul Mantz's red Boeing 100 and his Stinson trimotor to the latest bombers and fighters as visiting aircraft. *F. Bamberger*

ately known as the "Taj Mahal." The lab itself was spacious, spotless and well equipped. My staff was very proficient. I also had many opportunities to expose Kodachrome slides with my Contax.

While World War II had ignited in Europe, we were an ocean away from the actual scene, still at peace. My duties were never dull and consisted of a wide variety, from supervising my own shop to being Officer of the Day (O.D.). One morning our very capable Public Relations Officer, Capt. Bill Nuckols, notified me that a new Hollywood motion picture was going to be filmed - in part - at Randolph Field. Entitled "I Wanted Wings", it would involve a great deal of air-to-air filming. Within a short time, a bright red Boeing Model 100 biplane landed in company with a rare Stinson Model R trimotor airliner carrying the Paul Mantz support staff. Mantz's aviation operation was based at what had become Lockheed Air Terminal in Burbank, California, where he had become the star of aviation motion picture filming. That single-seat Boeing was essentially identical to the Boeing P-12 Air Corps and F4B-1 Navy fighters which had been standard first-line fighters in America in the late 1920s into the early 1930s. This tough antique was actually one of the first prototypes of the famed Boeing P-12 fighters, and Mantz was the pilot. A special platform mounted between the landing gear struts held a standard motion picture camera used to film aerial scenes of all varieties. The motion picture was a financial success, and served a secondary purpose of being a recruiting film for the Army Air Forces.

As new bases sprouted almost everywhere in 1940 and 1941, cadres of experienced personnel were drawn from established bases to set operations in motion. I visited many areas in Texas where new facilities were set up and made photographs for official records. After the Thanksgiving Day had passed in 1941, several of my friends and I obtained permission to make a formation round trip flight to El Paso, Texas. We departed Randolph in three North American BT-14 trainers on Friday afternoon, 5 December 1941, and flew a loose formation, arriving at Biggs Field shortly before sunset. We all enjoyed the weekend in El Paso and Juarez, Mexico. On Sunday morning we departed Biggs Field for Randolph via Midland Army Air Field and NAS Hensley Field in Dallas. We were airborne somewhere between Midland and Dallas when we picked up a startling message that Japanese aircraft had attacked our military and naval bases at Pearl Harbor. Now, in a flash, it had all become too real and we Americans had been dragged into the maelstrom of actual conflict. It was obvious that life as we had known it was about to change radically

A mixture of confusion and anger besieged the country for weeks after the attacks on Pearl Harbor, installations in the Philippine Islands and Southeast Asia had taken place. On March 9th, 1942, the War Department itself was reorganized into three autonomous forces. They were the Army Air Forces, Ground Forces and Services of Supply. Knowing that my assignment could change in a moment, I requested leave to visit my parents who were in Florida for a vacation. Leave granted, I decided to 'hitchhike by air' to Florida, since one of my buddies could fly me to NAS New Orleans. We departed Randolph in a BT-14, flew on to Ellington Field in Houston where we were to refuel. As we taxied in to the Visiting Aircraft area, I could see a fair number of B-25 Mitchells parked on the flight line. In Operations I learned they were on a special training mission, scheduled to return to Eglin Field in the Florida Panhandle.

Venturing out to the B-25s, I spotted Ted Lawson, one of the pilots who was a friend of mine from flight training. I asked him if there was room aboard for a hitchhiker. He looked at me sort of strangely, then asked me, "Do you have your own 'chute?" Given an affirmative nod, he told me to "Get in my airplane right now!" In a couple of minutes I was able to grab my gear and double-time to the Mitchell. As soon as Lawson and the crew were aboard, I settled in behind him. He spoke over his shoulder to me. "This is a very sensitive mission and we're not supposed to have anyone aboard who is not a crew member." But having spotted my Contax camera, he added, "Okay, you're now the Official Photographer. If you get any good pictures, I hope you won't forget me."

That flight to Eglin was truly spectacular. Once the B-25Bs and C became airborne, they took up a loose formation, leveling off at 500 feet. They made one flyby over Ellington, then set a course for Florida, never exceeding that 500-foot altitude for the next several hours on the way to Eglin. According to the rules,

flying that low in a bomber on an extended cross-country not an acceptable procedure. Flat-hatting as we were did make for some great photographic opportunities and the faithful Contax performed admirably. Nearing the Pensacola area, the B-25 formation "tightened up" and dipped right down over the Gulf waves so that I felt I could reach the whitecaps. We touched down smoothly, thus ending one of the most memorable flights I have ever experienced.

That training mission did have a special purpose, but I had no idea what it was all about. My mental questions were answered a short time later - on April 18, 1942 to be exact - when these same aircraft bombed Tokyo. I had been part of the last practice mission for the Doolittle attack from an aircraft carrier on the Japanese homeland. (Fred's unparalleled Kodachrome exposures from that last practice mission appear in this volume and in my WWII Pacific War Eagles book. Nobody on the actual mission ever brought back air-to-air color photographs! - Ed.)

Upon my return to Randolph Field, I learned that I had been transferred into Headquarters, Gulf Coast Training Command, just one of a few stateside assignments I had before heading overseas. That final stateside reporting point was Jefferson Barracks, Missouri, where I was to prepare for immediate overseas shipment. At the departure point, Camp Patrick Henry, Virginia, I was designated as Shipment Commander and learned that we were headed for North Africa. Before long we found ourselves aboard a British Lend-Lease Liberty ship, the S.S. Sambay, loaded with ammunition, bombs and high-octane aviation gasoline. Five other officers and I comprised the "troops" aboard, all headed for Gibraltar. After a hazardous voyage punctuated by Luftwaffe attacks, we landed safely in North Africa. In due time, the combat situation for the Allied Forces began to progress favorably and, as the war moved northward, I found myself in Naples, Italy, where I was directed to report to the commander of the 90th Photo Recon Wing, Familiarization with the area and current operational activities was the order of the day, and I again found myself as a student, this time to the Mediterranean Allied Photo Recon School. I soon gained a deep appreciation of how effective up-to-the-minute combat intelligence was toward the attainment of military objectives. In the course of many events, I received orders to report to the Commanding General of the Twelfth Air Force. Traveling with my B-4 bag and the trusty Contax, I reported to Headquarters as ordered. To my great surprise, I learned that the 12th Air Force Headquarters had no photo section at all, and that elements of the nearby 90th Photo Recon Wing was supporting them. Assigned to the Public Relations Section temporarily, I was given the designation of "Official War Photographer." They then sent me out on inspection tours to the combat units in the area, with instructions to make photographs for news releases and official records. Upon returning to Hq., I was summoned to the CG's office and told to set up a photo section as quickly as possible. Trying to find necessary personnel and equipment in the combat zone proved to be a task of no small proportion.

Eventually I received a call from the CG's secretary, requiring my appearance at headquarters. M/Gen. J. K. Cannon was in a good mood as he said, "Lieutenant, I just got word that a shipment of new photographic equipment has arrived at our depot in North Africa. Take an airplane, head down there and see if there is anything you can use. The Adjutant General will provide necessary orders to cover your actions." Then managing a sly smile, he quietly said, "And one more thing, effective right now, you are hereby promoted to the rank of Captain." He personally pinned a new set of "tracks" on the collar of my shirt as I stood there trying to believe this was really happening. (It goes to prove that rank has its privileges. - Ed.) With such ultimately impressive support, the new photo section came into being rather quickly as an integral part of headquarters.

As the war progressed, I concluded that I must have had one of the most satisfying assignments imaginable, constantly moving about in the Mediterranean Theater of Operations on photographic and inspection tours at the command level. It was a fact that Kodachrome film processing required special chemicals and strict temperature control and handling. This was nearly impossible to achieve in the places where we had to work. Therefore, all of the Kodachrome film I exposed while overseas had to be transported to Eastman Kodak in the U.S. for processing. Of course I arranged to have my own Contax 35-mm film slides diverted to my parents for storage. As a result, I never saw any of the unofficial color photographs I took until I returned to New York years later. My old friend at the camera shop, source of the Contax camera, was able to supply 35mm Kodachrome film - which was only rationed by availability - to my parents. It always arrived at the overseas destination in good condition. (It is easy to see why Fred Bamberger is such an asset to the historical archive of aviation lore, although largely unrecognized in comparison to such greats as Rudy Arnold, Hans Groenhoff and Alfred Steichen. As an author and publisher, I am privileged to have known Freddie for decades, aware of his talents. - Auth.)

I probably received the greatest compliment of my career many years later when I was having breakfast with retired Brigadier General George W. Goddard in Boca Raton, Florida. The General has long been recognized as the Godfather of Air Corps photographic operations. He was no less an authority on the use of color film in aviation. He said to me, "Freddie, not only have your Kodachromes retained their brilliant colors, but your slides of Army Air Forces activities and aircraft in the Mediterranean Theater of Operations are some of the best I have ever seen come out of World War II." Who could wish for any greater accolade than that?

Having long association with Warren Bodie, especially in the creation of two books of his own conception, WWII WAR EAGLES and WWII PACIFIC WAR EAGLES. I know that these books about America's fabulous Arsenal of Democracy will be beautiful books of the highest quality.

Fred E. Bamberger, Jr.
Colonel, USAF (Ret.)

NOTE: Just a few days after I talked by telephone with Fred, I learned from his daughter that he passed away quietly on Oct. 31, 1999, at the age of 83. All three volumes of a trio of WWII AMERICAN WAR EAGLES books will stand as a silent tribute to this gentleman because all will feature many of his color slides from WWII. - *Ed.*

Although it was after the Pearl Harbor sneak attack, Fred had reason enough to photograph this NAA BT-9A dead center over the Randolph Field roundel. It was flanked with living quarters, school buildings and parallel rows of hangars. The field construction had been authorized (before the stock market crash of 1929) for the Air Corps, which was, itself, comparatively new – an outgrowth of the Army Air Service. *Bamberger*

Near the peak of the Depression of the 1930s, Donald Douglas and his engineers realized they had not gone quite far enough with the DC-2 design. They gambled and moved forward with the well-timed, well-designed DC-3/DST airliner. Young newcomer "Kelly" Johnson, Robert Gross, Willis Hawkins and others at tiny Lockheed Aircraft in Burbank saw the need for more speed and turned to development of the Model 14 Super Electra. They were not going to go head-to-head with Douglas as did designers in England, France, Italy and other countries. Capital was not plentiful, so the Model 14 was not likely to be a roaring success, but it found its own niche. Strangely, distant Japan became a good customer for the airliner, helping to keep Lockheed afloat with orders for 30 Model 14-G3s. Entrepreneur-aviator Howard Hughes did much to brighten the picture by circling the globe at the controls of a Super Electra in the record time of 91 hrs.14 minutes elapsed time in July 1938. His Model 14-N2 unfailingly covered a distance of 14,672 miles. Lockheed then moved on to design a "stretched" version as the Model 18 Lodestar. It appeared just about three weeks after war erupted in Europe. Hundreds of Lodestars like this Alaska Star Airlines sleek beauty served civilian and military operators during WWII. The type showed its real stature when Lockheed-Vega spawned Ventura, B-34, B-37, PV-1 and PV-2 military and naval aircraft from the basic design.   *Lockheed*

16

Chapter1

Life with a Sleeping Giant 1939 - 1941

With World War I fast slipping into the memory bank, the decade of the Twenties was a major period of adjustment. The automobile, airplanes, rapid changes in housing designs, an era of new skyscraper buildings and the "talking motion pictures" becoming a standard, prosperity beckoned. Prohibition, with liquor outlawed, brought on a flood of illegal activity never before encountered since the lawless days of the far west. Perhaps it was a coincidence, but Charles Lindbergh's solo flight across the Atlantic Ocean seemed to bring on a headlong dash toward industrial expansion, especially in the new field of aviation. The stock market on Wall Street soared in what seemed to be an endless climb to wealth and prosperity. Airplanes of virtually every shape, size and construction came to market in great proliferation. It seemed like Utopia.

At the same time, anything to do with the conduct of war became repulsive to Americans. Though this nation saw no destruction of property on the American continent, the people reacted as if massive destruction had been seen in every city. Naturally there was little support for expansion and modernizing this nation's military and naval forces. In that decade, the people only wanted to have a hilariously good time, buy a car or two, and make money in the stock market. Statesmen and politicians seemed only too happy to sign treaties aimed at limiting machines of war, seemingly forgetting that treaties have always been something to disregard when they no longer valid from their viewpoint. In this environment, the country's leading proponent of air power, Gen. William Mitchell, was "cashiered" from the U.S. Army. The power structure and political expediency would no longer tolerate the man's visionary thinking. The naval forces managed to hold their own, but the Army slowly began to wither on the vine. Nobody seemed to notice. The Army Air Corps was left in the proverbial dust by private and commercial aviation following Lindbergh's feat of bravery and skill in 1927. Military and naval rivalry, especially for funding, combined with antiquated thinking about the conduct of wars among senior officers. Political expediency was a major factor in retarding any expansion of our national defense forces. America slowly but surely slid to the point of being at least a fifth-or sixth-rate air power

in the world, and that was without even the slightest military intelligence about what was happening in Japan, a terribly secretive society. In actual fact, with respect to Russia and Japan, the USA was probably even lower in rating. The Japanese fighting airplanes were being combat tested, while the Army brass looked upon our fighters as being primarily for show. Our Douglas B-18 bombers, in a combat atmosphere, would have fared as badly as the RAF's Fairey Battles did in the Battle of France in 1940. That was total disaster.

The American industrial capacity in January 1939 far exceeded its actual use. The Midwest part of the country suffered tremendous losses because of the dust bowl conditions in Oklahoma and adjacent states. Cars did not sell well at all. Thousands of people who had lost their homes in the midst of the Great Depression were hardly inclined to buy new houses. Railroads, in particular, were in very poor financial shape, resulting in numerous failures. Strikes were seen everywhere, especially in the automotive industry and coal mines. Retail sales were in the doldrums. The aircraft industry was no better off until 1938 when the French and British orders for specific military aircraft were signed.

With war in Europe virtually guaranteed in early 1939, and a fact in September, America's total military force (Army, Navy and Marines) totaled 334,473 men (almost exclusively), less than 3 percent of the total personnel count of 12,123,455 in 1945. It is virtually a certainty that the military and naval forces were up to authorized strength in 1939 because it was a haven from unemployment. While governmental figures for unemployment were probably far from accurate in the 1930s, at its peak the number of workers without a job totaled 25,000,000 at a time when total U.S. population was not much over 110,000.000. Many state employees in the country were paid with pseudo money called scrip, nothing more than a promissory note with no backing to it.

It was a time when our military tank corps was called mechanized cavalry. In fact, regular cavalry was considered an elite organization, very highly respected. Our best battle tank was the virtually unknown M2. Existing only in small numbers, it at least served as the basic vehicle for the M3A Lee and Grant tanks

17

rushed into production to meet the needs of the British tank corps. Those orders actually forced the construction of the Chrysler Tank Arsenal near Detroit, Michigan, because the Army's primary tank arsenal lacked any real ability to mass-produce such vehicles.

Numbers convey an understandable status to the general public, but they do not define or relate to combat capabilities. For example, in 1933 (but extending into 1934), the Army Air Corps took delivery of its first production monoplane fighters, 111 Boeing P-26A "Peashooters" and 25 of the P-26B models. Late in the year, they received the first four of an order for 54 Consolidated PB-2 type fighters. That sounds real good until you realize that the Boeings were wire-braced-wing monoplanes with fixed landing gears, not retractable. Only the four P-30s delivered had retractable landing gears and cantilever wings. But wait…there's more! The other 50, to be delivered in 1935 as Consolidated P-30As, were essentially modifications of a Detroit-Lockheed 2-seat pursuit tested way back in 1932. They were big, weighing in at 5,000 lbs., some 2,000 more than the P-26As that were just as fast, there two years earlier and far more maneuverable. No more 2-seat fighters were ever accepted for production by the USAAF.

Now, while the USN started to get new fighters with retractable landing gears in 1934, as of the Fiscal Year 1940 (June) they only had received ONE production monoplane fighter! Not a fighter *type*, just a single F2A-1. By the end of 1940, only one year before Pearl Harbor, the Commander Aircraft in the Fleet Battle Force had only *ten* monoplane fighters, all Brewster F2A-1s, soon to prove their inferiority as naval fighters. Certainly the USN had many monoplanes, but all of them were P2Y or PBY flying boats, NJ and SNJ trainers and an assortment of utility-class aircraft (non-combat). A few of them were actually faster than the carrier-based fighter biplanes that constituted our aircraft carrier defensive force. Perhaps worse, two big experimental 4-engine flying boat patrol bombers were barely slower than all of our standard shipboard fighter biplanes.

Was any parent of a naval aviator or enlisted pilot ever told that even if that flier was at the controls of a first-line navy monoplane BT-1 dive bomber or TBD-1 torpedo bomber *not carrying a bomb or torpedo*, it would be no faster than one of their SNJ-2 training planes? Any Japanese spy could have learned that from public information. Is it any wonder that Japan felt very confident about sending new Mitsubishi A6M2 Reisen Type 0 Model 21s (Zero carrier fighter) against what was known to be available at Hawaii?

(Most Americans, immediately following the Japanese assaults on our Pacific islands, were contemptuous of our Asiatic opponents, but I can state with honesty that was not true of this [then] teenager, already employed in the defense industry while trying desperately to become a flying cadet. At that same time, my father – a WWI veteran – was a ranking employee of the Office of Production Management, the OPM. Within weeks of the Japanese attack, he was commissioned a Major in the new USAAF.)

This chapter reveals in original Kodachrome I color, some of it dating back to 1937, what any one of you – had you been there – would have seen if you were really lucky enough to have traveled to various places. That wonderfully stable color film, like Technicolor motion picture film, was not within reach of many of us at the time. The film and processing, not to mention cameras with good lenses, were truly expensive in a period when gasoline was available for as little as ten cents a gallon. Just be aware that some of these exposures have been exposed to indifferent-to-careless handling, unfriendly storage conditions and bad climatic environments. This book opens with an extremely rare photograph of a Seversky SEV-3M-WW military amphibian delivered to the Colombian government in 1936! Indeed, this actual exposure may have been made in 1936 rather than 1937. If this particular airplane was No.1 of three, it was first flown in August 1935. As the picture caption explains, it was taken on a river in Colombia, South America.

This volume concludes with the most remarkable color photograph we have ever encountered. It is an example of photographer bravery and excellent exposure under the dramatic conditions in the East Loch of Pearl Harbor on December 7, 1941, when the Japanese attack was still progressing. (Personally, I can never look at it without a lump rising in my throat.) Research has indicated that the Kodachrome as exposed was never before printed in color. Not even in National Geographic Magazine.

During the Battle of Britain in 1940, the U.S. Army Air Corps dispatched Col. Carl "Tooey" Spaatz and Capt. Ben Kelsey to England to evaluate aircraft design, performance and tactics. Missions accomplished, they returned to American shores to brief Air Corps generals ranging from top officer Gen. Hap Arnold to all senior officers involved from combat to procurement. At Wright Field, Ohio, Gen. Oliver Echols and his staff established the criteria for a new fighter that should be able to defeat the best that Germany's *Luftwaffe* could field. Republic Aviation's key personnel (including "Sasha" Kartveli, v.p. and chief designer) were called in and commissioned to develop a new pursuit (fighter) plane. Specifications and a contract were issued by the Army to initiate necessary action. The effects of the European evaluation tour were to have momentous impact on world history. Republic Aviation was the direct outgrowth of Seversky Aircraft, created in 1930 by Russian expatriate Major Alexander P. de Seversky, previously a close associate of Gen. Billy Mitchell in the U.S. Army Air Service after WWI. Seversky Aircraft's first military aircraft product was a trio of export fighter-recon amphibians identified as model SEV-3M-WW, based on his first company product, the SEV-3 civil aircraft. The Colombian government ordered three of them in the mid '30s. Shown here in full Colombian service markings is one of those military amphibians undergoing minor repair, probably on the R. Cauca near Barranquilla, Colombia. (This is the earliest known Kodachrome airplane photograph – c.1937 – to be taken outside the U.S.A.; in fact no photograph of a SEV-3M-WW with full Colombian military markings has been seen previously.) The pilot is presumed to be Colombia's technical advisor and test pilot Roger Q. Williams. The lady in the aft cockpit is thought to be his wife. But for the inventiveness and boundless energy of Alex Seversky, there would not have been a Seversky Aircraft Company with its unique products. And it follows there would never have been a Republic Aviation Corp. to produce its evolutionary P-47 Thunderbolt design. That design was based on the Seversky-Gregor wing configuration and the Major's turbosupercharger installation concept, first seen in the Seversky AP-4 military pursuit tested by the Air Corps in 1938. There is, therefore, a direct connection between the Seversky SEV-3M-WW and America's eventual Arsenal of Democracy product, the Thunderbolt. *D. Veres via G. Beauchamp.*

TOP: After several years of the Great Depression, America seemed to be on the road to economic recovery when the slide began again with the recession of 1937-39. A tiny U.S. Navy Reserve organization was staffed with weekend pilots and obsolescent aircraft like this Curtiss O2C-1 (formerly F8C-2) Helldiver, then serving as an observation aircraft. Seen here at the southwestern tip of New York's Long Island in 1937 is an O2C-1 operating from Floyd Bennett Field naval reserve air station. At least two Helldivers flew with a less famous Berliner-Joyce OJ-2 from that airport. (B-J was one of the failed companies which amalgamated into North American Aviation.) These "stick, cloth and wire" biplanes may have been state-of-the-art military aircraft just a handful of years earlier, but results of the stock market crash had taken their toll on new aircraft procurement, so these had to do. By comparison, Adolf Hitler – *Der Fuhrer* of Nazi Germany – was sending some of his new Messerschmitt Bf 109B-1 and –2 fighters to Spain for dueling with Russian Polikarpov I-15 and I-16 fighters flown by the Loyalists.

Although the advanced Bf 109Bs could boast only about 680 horsepower at that time (1937-38), they could attain a speed of at least 265 mph, far faster than the Air Corps' standard Boeing P-26 pursuit planes. Even more importantly, the Germans were rotating pilots and crews of the Condor Squadron in and out to gain significant combat training. (At that same time, U.S. Army commanders viewed pursuit planes as "crowd pleasers" at air shows, but they were considered far less important than observation, attack and bombing aircraft.) In the same era, Navy Grumman F2F and F3F biplane fighters were prime defensive fighters for our aircraft carriers, hardly more. One Army Air Corps pursuit group of brand new Seversky P-35 pursuit planes were in the process of replacing the P-26s at only one base, Selfridge Field, Michigan. But with 300 more horsepower, the Severskys were only 20 to 30 mph faster than the earliest service Bf 109s, and 77 was the total number of P-35s on order. America could hardly be proud of being at least a fifth-rate airpower, barely rated ahead of Portugal. It was probably worse since nobody could properly evaluate Japanese air power. Approximately 210 new Curtiss P-36As, while only a tad faster than the P-35s on the same power, were on order. First deliveries were scheduled for April 1938. Having come into complete power in Germany in 1933, Hitler was rapidly creating a devastatingly powerful war machine. But, of course. America had wide oceans at both ends to deter aggression. France had chosen a Socialist government, ultimately throwing their aircraft and war machine industry into socialized disarray. The British, having at least become aware of the threat of the Nazis, started late and were lucky to have had designers create the Spitfire and Hurricane interceptors. One bright spot appeared in the U.S.A. in 1936: Young Lieutenant Benjamin Kelsey, the Air Corps Fighter Projects Officer, defied convention and laid down specifications which led to the design and procurement of the radical Lockheed XP-38. Kelsey had magnificent foresight. He was one of our unsung heroes. *Fred Bamberger*

RIGHT With the American economy still mired deep in the Great Depression of the '30s decade, the U.S. Congress made incredibly bad decisions concerning procurement of defensive aircraft. In a fateful order to procure the largest numerical count of aircraft for the funds allocated to the Department of the Army, the Douglas DB-2 (or XB-18) bomber was selected to replace the aging Martin B-10/B-12 fleet. It was quite obvious that the competing Boeing 299X (XB-17) had to be scored far above the B-18 type in everything except low price per copy, but technology evidently was not in the lexicon of the American Congress. The 299X had 2.5 times more defensive firepower, even in its prototype configuration, than any B-18. Inherent in the design was far greater speed and range and probably ten times the capability for modernization of design. Most certainly, some of the congressional thinking was impacted by an accident which destroyed the Boeing prototype at Wright Field during the testing phase. Pilot error resulted in a takeoff attempt with the flight controls locked. That was a pre-"Murphy's Law" accident if ever there was one. With reference to production B-18 defensive armament, there were only two useful positions, each armed with one puny .30-cal. machine gun in an un-powered turret – not one iota better than that of a Martin B-10. Side and top protection was in the form of one .30-cal. weapon in a retractable turret. With the turret raised, drag was increased nearly equaling the effects of extending the landing gear. In a critical defensive mode in combat, the B-18 would have been no faster than a DC-3 airliner at cruise. Despite the realities, Contract AC-8307 issued on Feb. 2, 1936, was for 82 Douglas bombers, and 51 more were procured on contract amendments. In a gesture most likely aimed at keeping Boeing from closing its doors, a contract for 13 service test Y1B-17s was approved on Jan. 17, 1936. By the time the first B-18s were being delivered on the production contract, Germany was putting the Condor Squadron into combat in Spain – on behalf of Gen. Francisco Franco – equipped with new, powerfully armed Messerschmitt Bf 109D fighters. The obese B-18s and newer B-18As (with tiny improvements) were the mainstays of the Army Air Corps bomber force when Germany started WWII with the invasion of Poland in September 1939. Meanwhile, newer production Boeing B-17C/D versions of the "Flying Fortress" were capable of flying at altitudes never even envisioned for the B-18 series, and at far greater speeds. Yet, even the B-17D was proven to be obsolete at the time as most of them were being dispatched to our first lines of defense in the Pacific. Newer, far more potent B-17Es were being developed. All B-18s would have been flying coffins if used in any real combat theater of action. Many went to the Canadians as trainers. A few were eventually assigned to RCAF anti-submarine squadron duty and the new USAAF converted some to B-18Bs with pioneering sub-hunting electronic equipment.

OPPOSITE   In addition to the Curtiss O2C-1s, the reservists also flew Berliner-Joyce OJ-2s like the biplane at the far right. They were directly related to early 1930s Air Corps observation airplanes such as the Douglas O-38B series. The B/J company was formed not long after the stock market crash in 1929 part of a large holding company. A few prototype fighters were built for the U.S. Navy, but their only production contract was for an Army two-seat fighter biplane designated P-16 and the OJ-2 naval observation planes. Those OJ types could be flown with wheel landing gear or floats. A merger of Fokker-Atlantic, B/J and other assets resulted in formation of General Aviation, largely owned by General Motors Corporation. In 1934, the new Airmail Act forced the parent corporation to divest its non-manufacturing aviation assets to concentrate only on aircraft manufacturing. The Dundalk, Maryland, plant was developing a single-engine transport, a new NA-16 basic trainer and the GA-15 observation plane. Management was reorganized with James 'Dutch' Kindelberger as president. A decision was made to move to California and build a new plant there. North American's new factory was built at the intersection of Imperial Highway and Aviation Blvd. on or adjacent to Mines Field property (now Los Angeles International/LAX). Therefore, the B/J OJ Navy aircraft outlived the company that built them. The '30s were a very tough, decade, financially speaking. Located across the highway from the Douglas El Segundo plant, the new North American Aviation factory was a big improvement over the 1920s Dundalk facility. Under leadership of Kindelberger and Chief Engineer Leland Atwood, the trainer and observation planes were designed and developed, becoming the NA-15/BT-9 and XO-47 respectively. For a time, NAA had survived by manufacturing float sets for Curtiss SOC-1 scout planes being built in the east. The BT-9 trainer led to an entire family of the most famous trainers in the world, and the GA/NA-15 design led to 164 orders for O-47 observation aircraft. By some major stroke of luck or vision, NAA came into being even as war loomed on the far horizon.   *Fred Bamberger*

As the Great Depression weighed ever more heavily on Americans with each passing month and year, unemployment soared to levels that even government statisticians could not begin to cope with. For example, U.S. Steel Corporation, a pillar of American industry, laid off some 225,000 workers in a relatively short time span. Aircraft manufacturers tumbled into oblivion like tenpins. Powerful railroads that had astronomical earnings for decades and carried stupendous political clout collapsed. Little Northrop Corp. struggled to survive at its El Segundo, California, location close by Mines Field. Engineer Don Berlin was closely associated with Ed Heinemann on the Northrop XFT-1 and improved -2 Navy fighter, and on design of a new derivative for the Army Air Corps competition in 1935. Their only hope was to use the existing XFT tooling and try to modernize the design. Greatest improvements were in the NACA cowling for the P&W R-1535 engine, probably the most powerful unit they dared install on the tiny fighter, and elimination of the trademark 'pant-like' landing gear fairings. Those famous trousers were highly favored by John Northrop, but the time had come to abandon them. Incredibly, the change was a quantum leap forward to a minimal-drag retractable landing gear. Unfortunately, the aircraft disappeared into the Pacific Ocean on a perfectly clear day. In the meantime, Northrop had a terminal argument with Don Berlin, resulting in the latter's departure. Berlin was available to end the quest for a project design engineer at Curtiss-Wright's airplane division in Buffalo, NY. Once again, he was working on a pursuit aircraft to compete for a fighting machine replacement for the then current first-line Boeing P-26s, rapidly approaching obsolescence. He was immediately assigned to head up design of the Curtiss Model 75. Top management saddled him with a significant ground rule: the airplane must be powered with a Wright engine. The initial Wright SGR-1670-5 powerplant was not long in proving it was a 'dud' during initial flights of the Model 75 in 1935. *CONTINUED ON NEXT PAGE ....*

FROM PREVIOUS PAGE   Overall, the engine situation was so bad for all competitors, Lt. Benjamin Kelsey called a halt at the abysmal performance of all entries, postponing the contest until the following spring. Berlin eventually settled on using the Wright SR-1820-G Cyclone engine. Competing Seversky, with its SEV-1XP, made the same choice, but not for long. It proved to be an intolerable mating, so Major Seversky managed to borrow a new Pratt & Whitney R-1830 Twin Wasp from the manufacturer. He also wisely hired young engineer and military pilot C. Hart Miller to re-engine the SEV-1XP. The airplane was declared winner of the competition despite higher unit pricing, mainly because the Wright Cyclone was unable to reliably provide anything near its advertised power. Although the tiny Farmingdale, NY, company won a contract for 77 pursuit airplanes to be designated P-35, significant changes were demanded. (In private conversations, Gen. Ben Kelsey admitted making a serious mistake in not awarding a nominal service test contract for thirteen aircraft in order to develop a flush retractable landing gear, etc. However, Curtiss-Wright used its considerable political clout to allow Curtiss to submit three re-engined Model 75E Hawks with Pratt & Whitney engines for evaluation. They became Y1P-36 airplanes, soon to be followed by a contract for no less than 210 Curtiss P-36As, all utilizing the P&W R-1830 engines. While most of the fighters went to AAC groups in 1938, a small number remained at Wright Field and/or nearby Patterson Field for development testing. Those pursuit planes remained in natural aluminum (unpainted) finish even into post Pearl Harbor times, as did many other aircraft under test. Faced with Nazi movements in Europe, the French *Armee de l'Air* ordered hundreds of the Hawk H75-As because of impending war. This P-36A, believed to be piloted by Major Signa Gilkey out of Patterson Field, was typical of hundreds of Model 75 aircraft attributable to Don Berlin's engineering. Thousands of Curtiss P-40 and export H-81 versions were eventually built for WWII, powered by Allison and Rolls-Royce engines.   *Rudy Arnold (2)*

RIGHT   There is one military aircraft appropriately named. It brings to mind one Lockheed P-38 operated in the Far East during the war. It was named "My Assam Dragon" by the pilot. What the Douglas B-23 was draggin' (intentional faux pas) was the performance reputation and combat effectiveness of its parents, the B-18/B-18A team. With a few years of military service records available, the Project Office staff should have known that B-23s would be no more a threat to an enemy than its British Vickers Wellington III cousin (by marriage) was to Berlin. If anyone reads between the lines of pre-war thinking or sees a smoking gun in 1939, there is room to believe that the AAC was still bending to political pressure from Washington. The fate of M/Gen. Frank Andrews in February of that year for speaking the truth about our Air Corps stature was certainly a giant cannon shot of warning[2]. It is probable that others ran for cover, recommending the purchase of "improved" Douglas B-18s rather than make a large award to Boeing for improved B-17 bombers. A contract was issued for 38 of the new B-23 bombers, supposedly utilizing much of the B-18 tooling. In the long run, the only components that might have commonality were the outer wing panels and perhaps the landing gear. At approximately the same time, the AAC ordered 39 Boeing B-17Bs featuring turbosuperchargers and other

improvements. Notice the purchase quantity similarity. The B-23, even with two new Wright R-2600 engines rated at 1600 hp each, was just another slow bomber compared with the contemporary B-17B. The Dragon was 15 tons gross weight against 24 tons gross weight, and the B-17B was faster, carried a larger bomb load, had greater range and flew much higher. Even with those attributes, the B-17B, C and D models were hardly fully combat worthy. The Dragon would have been mince meat. Defensive armament aboard the B-23 was, at best, no better than armament on the Vickers Wellingtons. It must be remembered that Wellingtons flew mostly after dark. The Army Air Corps had no real training program for night bombing operations. It is easy to get the impression that the Arnold-Eaker team was so enamored of the Norden bomb sight that they never even considered 10-tenths overcasts. Specifications leading to the B-23 bomber appear to have been badly flawed in concept. A casual look at the North American XB-21 reveals it was not a bit more advanced than the Douglas design, perhaps less so. Both were losers in any combat environment. Soon after the Pearl Harbor debacle, a dozen B-23's were logically transformed into UC-67s, relegating them to non-combat cargo carrying work. The others may have been assigned to anti-submarine patrol work for a time, but ultimately wound up as bomber-trainers.   *Robert D. Archer Coll.*

[2]Gen. Andrews was Chief of the GHQ Air Force as 1939 opened. In January he spoke at the annual convention of the National Aeronautics Assoc., saying that "the U.S. is a 5th or 6th rate air power". He also stated that his combat organization of the Army Air Corps (the GHQ Air Force) "has only 400+ fighting planes." He was soon dispatched to purgatory.

 LEFT   Although the year 1937 cannot be considered as a vintage year in any sense of the word, it sets the scene to illustrate how America made such a tremendous, stupendous leap forward from the doldrums of the Great Depression to become the true Arsenal of Democracy. It was also a year punctuated by the appearance of a most radical fighting plane, the Bell XFM-1 Airacuda. Compared to French multi-seat fighters, this airplane seemed designed for Buck Rogers at the time. Lt. Ben Kelsey was the chosen pilot to test the new fighter for Bell Aircraft since they did not have a qualified test pilot. Bell had produced what was most likely the first military aircraft designed around the new Allison V-1710 engine. While the XFM-1 appeared to be state-of-the-art or better, it had some serious design flaws. For example, the airfoil chosen mirrored the older, slower Curtiss Y1A-18. The gun stations in front of the pusher engines offered no escape route for the two gunners. In a proposal contest involving hundreds of points, it only outdid the Lockheed XFM-2 by a single point. For outmoded reasons, the landing gear wheels protruded like those on the B-17 and B-18 heavy bomber designs, creating drag. A service test quantity of twelve YFM-1s – the version shown here – was ordered, ultimately separated into three entities. One model was fitted with a tricycle landing gear, currently coming into mode. Gunners were to be omitted from the nacelle stations equipped with Browning M-4 37-mm cannons, with firing to be controlled by the second pilot. That could have been a handicap in repelling mass frontal attacks. (A second sighting station was needed on top for better cannon control.) The entire concept of multi-seat fighters was controversial, eventually leading – in part – to the resignation of Capt. Claire Chennault. He was a determined voice, along with Kelsey, against multi-seat fighters. As it turned out in WWII, pinpoint bombing with the Norden bombsight in combat environment turned out to be a myth. The British Bomber Command soon learned that night bombing was just as ineffective when the bulk of their targets (even cities) were missed by miles, not feet. With a laminar-flow wing, 1700 hp vee engines, and perhaps a brace of 20 or 30-mm cannons in each nacelle, no co-pilot but top and bottom sighting stations for two gunners, the type might well have served better than the Bell P-39 Airacobra. Only experience would have told.   *Bell Aircraft*

RIGHT & OPPOSITE BELOW   Summer, 1939, was quite pleasant overall. The all-pervading labor unrest in America had relaxed a bit, although John L. Lewis was as hard-nosed in dealing with companies as ever. The C.I.O. union had raised hob with the major steel companies, mining companies and of course the automobile industry. Overseas, Hitler's Nazis were generally driving the more democratic countries of Europe to the point of total exasperation. In the Far East, Japan carried unrelenting warfare to China, and there were continuing border wars with Russia. One thing almost totally overlooked in the 1930s in America was the reconstruction, modernization and construction of airbases and other military/naval facilities. Selfridge Field, Michigan, was a classic example. Modern hangars and shops replaced the WWI ramshackle buildings. Living facilities were mostly new brick buildings. With few exceptions, airplanes seen on the field were primarily Curtiss P-36As and Cs plus virtually all of the Seversky P-35s serving the Army Air Corps. One other thing rarely mentioned during the '30s, was the program aimed at developing a satisfactory aircraft camouflage scheme. Fairly large numbers of airplanes involved in maneuvers from early in the decade – the largest being the Boeing XB-15 – were swathed with (mostly) water-based paint. Easily applied and removed, a variety of earth colors were applied. With John Q. Public in mind, First Pursuit Group P-36Cs appearing at the Cleveland National Air Races in 1939 bore the latest in camouflage paint schemes. Pictured on the ground and in the air at Selfridge Field, these Curtiss P-36Cs (modified A pursuits) were certainly distinctive. Evidently, no two were alike. Since co-production was possible with the Air Corps contract for 210 of the Curtiss Hawks, the government released the type for export. With war fears mounting in Europe as the Spanish Civil War roared on, the French *Armee de l'Air* was faced with a serious dearth of combat-quality aircraft. They turned to America in 1938 for hundreds of Curtiss Hawk H75-A fighters because nationalization of the aircraft industry had created chaos in France. Once deemed the best air power in the world, it had slid alarmingly to a much lower stature. The first-line fighter force in 1940 consisted primarily of Morane-Saulnier M.S. 406s, essentially a 1935 design featuring engines rated at less than 900 horsepower. As 1940 moved toward summer, America's president was asking for 50,000 airplanes a year. Late in 1938, the target rate of French aircraft production was 2500 a year, with industry struggling to attain 40-50 percent of that target rate. American engines supplied unmatched reliability at the close of the decade. It is notable that the first *Armee de l'Air* combat victories over *Luftwaffe* fighters came on 9 Sept. 1939 when five Curtiss H75-A1s tangled with five Messerschmitt Bf 109Es. Two German planes were shot down without any French losses.   *Army Air Corps*

LEFT Boeing Airplane Company was awarded a contract for one prototype VHB (Very Heavy Bomber), the XB-15,when they were known as a builder of Army and Navy fighter aircraft. On a smaller scale, Boeing built passenger aircraft and had delivered a handful of modern monoplane 2-engine bombers to the Air Corps. Martin had won large contracts for their B-10 and B-12 bombers which were radical improvements over any bomber type in the world. For the VHB competition, Martin had envisioned a huge 6-engine bomber powered by the new Allison engines. That radical aircraft had a wing spread of 173 feet. But this time, Boeing was the winner with their large XB-15 design. Compared to foreign bombers, it was extremely advanced in concept. What really made it significant was the ability to cruise over a maximum range of more than 5000 miles, a statistic unheard of in those days. With a wing spanning 149 feet, it was larger than any bomber in the world. Unfortunately, it was handicapped by Pratt & Whitney R-1830-11 engines producing only 950 horsepower each.However, considering what the British, French, Germans and Italians had in development testing in 1937, the XB-15 was far advanced in concept and creation. "Old Grandpappy", as she was named, is depicted here in experimental camouflage paint, most likely in the winter of 1939 at Langley Field, VA. Two ranking officers are seen in their Winter Dress Blues escorting three pretty women on a tour of the base. During much of WWII, first as the XB-15 and then as the XC-105, the bomber carried cargo from Miami Army Air Field, FL, and Kelly Field, TX, to Panama, CZ, as part of the Air Transport Command. *Army Air Corps.*

RIGHT   Much to the distress of all concerned, from 1939 until today, no photographs of the prototype Lockheed XP-38 on the ground were taken in color, and not even one black & white photograph of the airplane in flight has ever surfaced. Of course Lockheed was a "small potatoes" aircraft company trying hard to sell their Model 14 Super Electra airliners, and the Model 22 – company designation for the XP-38 – had frightening cost overruns attributable to their military airplanes, since Lockheed was rescued from bankruptcy in 1932. In fact it was only its second such aircraft in the history of the organization. A young lieutenant named Benjamin Kelsey, the Air Corps' Fighter Projects Officer, had laid out the radically advanced specifications for a 2-engine fighter in 1935-36. Another brilliant young engineer, C. L. "Kelly" Johnson, was on the same wavelength and won the competition for Lockheed with his radical design in 1937. Kelsey was selected to make the first flights in the prototype, and in February 1939 made a near record-breaking transcontinental flight from Burbank, CA, to Long Island, NY, exceeding a speed of 400 mph at times in the process. The prototype was forced to refuel twice at a leisurely pace en route because drop tanks had not been authorized for AAC fighters. During final leg letdown at Mitchel Field, NY, a handful of obsolete PB-2A fighters preceded him in the pattern because nobody thought to report this as a record flight to Mitchel officials. When power was needed at the last minute, the idling engines failed to respond and Kelsey crash landed on a golf course. Only one prototype had been built in those days of tight budgets. It became a Class 26 pile of scrap metal. This almost technically accurate painting depicting the XP-38 in flight is as close as anyone could get to the real thing in color. It appeared in Lockheed ads in several magazines.   *Lockheed Aircraft.*

LEFT   During the course of World War II, Allison Engineering Co. produced and delivered no fewer than 69,233 of their V-1710 liquid-cooled engines. Those figures do not include deliveries prior to January 1, 1940, because the agencies recording the data had no mandate to do the job. Allison was delivering a tiny series of experimental and development V-1710's since 1935, and they also delivered the 3420-cubic-inch displacement V-3420 engines in small numbers. It was a remarkable performance. What makes it even more astonishing was the fact that the entire project was initiated by the Army Air Corps in the depths of the Depression. As if that was not adequately impressive, the first V-1710 engine was not even flight tested in an airplane until Santa Claus time in 1936. Tiny Bell aircraft installed one in a Consolidated A-11A on a $25,000 contract from the Air Corps. That odd-looking "flying test bed" was flown by at least three different AAC test pilots, one of them being the Fighter Projects Officer, young Lt. Benjamin Kelsey who chalked up at least 100 hours on the aircraft. One other officer assigned to log lots of hours on the engine – a boring, sometimes dangerous job at best – was Lt. Mark E. Bradley. Both men eventually rose to the level of general officers in the AAF. The V-1710 had many detractors during the war, because of many blowups, but it is remarkable that we even had such a fine inline liquid-cooled engine in that war. It was the *one and only* mass-produced, turbosupercharged liquid-cooled engine manufactured by the Allies in the war. No version of the great Rolls-Royce Merlin was even adapted to turbosupercharging. America's top-scoring fighter aces in WWII flew Lockheed P-38 Lightnings, all powered by turbosupercharged Allison V-1710s. No fewer than 10,038 P-38 Lightnings rolled from production lines and each one was powered by two V-1710s. This early V-1710C series engine – with installed cooling radiators - was of the type used in the earliest Curtiss P-40 and Tomahawk fighters and the XP-38 prototype. It was easily identified by the long extension shaft case. In the last year of the war, the newest Allison V-1710 produced more than 1745 hp (WEP, War Emergency Power). Lockheed P-38s operated in every theater of the war, were by far the longest-ranging fighters to reach combat status, and they were the first Allied bomber-escort fighters to reach Berlin, Germany. Bar none!   *Jack Kerr via W. Thompson*

Normal peacetime yellow and black hangar roofs catch your eye, and that was exactly what was intended – for fliers – in the U.S.A. in the 1930s. It was difficult to know if you were at Selfridge Field, Michigan, or March Field, Calif., unless you looked at the landscape or the Operations office. In this case, the Curtiss P-36As were assigned to the 36th Pursuit Group based at Langley Field, Virginia, in 1940. While the Navy tried various low-visibility paint schemes instead of the ribald color markings of the biplane era, the Air Corps merely experimented with pseudo camouflage applied in water-soluble paint during most of the decade. That was an eye-catcher at the 1939 Cleveland National Air Races. In a more serious vein, the infantry-minded generals and staff officers looked at pursuit (fighter) aircraft as recruiting and public relations tools, not as indigenous components of a tactical weapon. They also engaged in bitter territorial battles with the Navy, especially when the Boeing Y1B-17s demonstrated ship interception far at sea. Remarkably progressive Maj. Gen. Frank M. Andrews – and not to forget, Brev. Gen. Billy Mitchell – lost his leadership position for speaking out about the sorry state of our air force in 1939. It must have been heartbreaking to be logical and dedicated, only to be kicked downstairs for telling the truth. Eventually, though, he was vindicated…something that did not come to Mitchell in his lifetime. Curtiss P-36s were handsome pursuit planes, but from a technical view they were based on 1934 (or earlier) technology. Struggling Curtiss-Wright Corp. "bought" a then-massive contract for 210 Curtiss P-36As in FY 1937 – a Recession year – by pricing the aircraft (w/o engine) at about $17,885 each. It would have been more logical to follow Ben Kelsey's desire to insist on updated Seversky P-35s with improvements demonstrated on the Major's much improved AP. In a classified AAC test report, signed by Capt. Stanley Umstead on June 8, 1937, the unsupercharged airplane had been formally clocked at 307.0 mph on only 900 horsepower. A newer P&W R-1830 engine was coming, guaranteeing a speed of at least 320 mph, right up there with the new RAF Hawker Hurricane Mk.I. Maj. Seversky drew the wrath of military brass by demonstrating the AP-2 to the public on Memorial Day at St. Louis. That combined with a slightly damaging landing at Floyd Bennett Field, NY, on Sept. 1 and the "bargain basement" price offered as incentive to buy P-36As was a disaster for Seversky Aircraft, not to mention the Major and his AP-2. It never flew again.   *AAC*

As the year 1930 staggered in, having been smote mightily by the crashing stock market, the chief of development engineering, Sam Heron, at Wright Field initiated a development program intended to produce high-horsepower aircraft engines. By direction, all of the contracts eventually awarded were for liquid-cooled engines using the newly formulated Prestone as coolant. Continental Motors received the initial contract for development of such an engine, launching what became a seemingly endless and non-productive program. Eventually it involved development programs with Continental, Lycoming, Chrysler and Wright Aero. The bomber people thought they could reduce aerodynamic drag on large aircraft by burying engines within thick bombing aircraft wings, not realizing that a severe price would be paid for other factors not considered. Air Corps personnel picked up the appellation "Hyper" from the Navy's parallel high-performance aircraft engine program, which was aimed entirely at development of Hyper (high-performance) air-cooled engines. Early in 1939, Wright proposed development of their new R-2160 liquid-cooled 42-cylinder radial engine. Official title at Wright Aero was Wright Tornado 617. By January 1941, they had a contract to develop ten Tornado engines in two distinct models at a price of $63,000 each. The AAC, soon to become AAF, intention was to use the new 2350 hp engines in Lockheed's XP-58, Republic's XP-69 and the proposed Hughes DX-2. Each engine comprised three segments of 14 radial cylinders each, all connected – but with no common crankshaft! The program wandered on for several years, constantly undergoing major changes. Among changes were use of a 2-speed engine gearbox, even with drive for single-rotation or dual-rotation propellers, plus optional right- or left-hand rotation. The R-2160 Tornado eventually became possibly the most complex aircraft engine ever built. Another Curtiss-Wright "success." Of course the engine type had to be suitable for use with turbosupercharging. Toward the end of 1940, yes 1940, after three segments were assembled into an engine that was run for one hour, the Chief, Experimental Engine Section (AAC), stated that "Some day the Tornado will be a beautiful engine for pursuit-type airplanes." By July 14, 1941, AAF chief Gen. H. H. Arnold directed Materiel Division to "try to get a (viable) Tornado engine installation by next July 4." (Independence Day, 1942.) As of February 1943, Lockheed had been waiting for the two necessary R-2160 engines since autumn 1942. By May 1943 there was " no need for these engines since the XP-58 had been equipped with 3000 hp Allison V-3420 engines. By February 1944, the government cancelled ten of the engines, but it cost them $630,000 in cancellation costs. By June 1945 all contracts were cancelled because "the Government no longer required the engines." As can be seen in these photographs, at least one R-2160 survived, and supposedly there were either three or five engines completed. None was ever flight tested! So much for AAF program management, and so much for Curtiss-Wright's typical performance in WWII. The last Hyper engine was Lycoming's monstrous 36-cylinder air-cooled radial engine, the XR-7755. It was the largest aircraft piston engine ever built. The displacement was seven thousand seven hundred and fifty-five cubic inches. That Lycoming weighed in at just over three tons. *Robert Coiro (3)*

For patently obvious reasons, Grumman A/C Engineering Corporation's new (in 1933) XF2F-1 prototype shipboard fighter was promptly referred to as the "Flying Barrel" in the press. Tiny, compact, fast and maneuverable for the era with a demonstrated speed of 230 mph, it immediately became the fastest of the world's carrier-based fighters by a wide margin. It was promptly adopted for production in 1934-35 in some of the worst Depression days. The F2F-1s were the world's first standard naval single-seat fighters to have retractable landing gear. Incredibly, they survived the rigors of seagoing operations, and ultimately training, well into the early 1940s. Even more remarkably, this single Kodachrome I image was recorded by a USN cadet aviator late in 1940. Somehow it survived unprotected for 60 years before discovery by the author. It is shown in full original 1940 official colors during its final first-line assignment to America's Neutrality Patrol. Coming from VF-7, it had just been assigned to NAS Miami, Florida, as a fighter and dive-bomber trainer. Apparently it had last served aboard the USS *Wasp* (CV-7), one of only two F2F-1s assigned to that newly commissioned carrier in 1940. Another twenty-one were still serving aboard USS *Lexington* (CV-2) as part of Carrier Division One.   *E. W. Simpson Jr.*

After years of seeing wonderfully colorful paint jobs on USN aircraft, most of that was to come to a hesitant halt as 1941 dawned. A BuAer directive was issued on 30 December 1940, ordering that all ship-based aircraft would be painted a non-reflective light grey color. Fleet patrol aircraft would be painted similar blue-grey on the upper surfaces and light grey on the underside. All markings were eventually to be added in insignia white. This Vought SB2U-3 assigned to USMC squadron VMSB-131 (formerly VMS-1) was duly painted according to that directive which, itself, was modified according to a new one issued 26 February 1941. The new designators reflected creation of two Marine Aircraft Wings, one Quantico-based, the other based at NAS San Diego on San Diego Bay, California. The base is possibly the largest U.S. Naval Air Station in the world, and its actual location is on North Island, officially known also as "The Birthplace of Naval Aviation." (Because of dredging and filling operations, the base is no longer on an island, just part of Coronado at the northern end of the Silver Strand.) *USMC/NA*

In a delightful time warp situation, we are suddenly and unexpectedly carried back six decades from the millennial year 2000 to this view of a formation of Grumman F3F-3 Navy fighters in formation over San Diego County, California. The occasion was the making of a motion picture, "Dive Bomber," starring Errol Flynn and Fred MacMurray. This flight of F3F-3s, the final version of the barrel-shaped biplanes that first appeared in the early 1930s, belonged to squadron VF-5 assigned to the USS *Yorktown* (CV 5). That gallant lady was a major element in that Thin Grey Line of carriers which fought so vigorously in the Pacific to fend off the early Imperial Japanese Navy onslaught in WWII. While the ship was in port in 1940, the Grummans were based at NAS North Island, by then part of Coronado Island. If any airplane in the world had charisma, the F3F was leading the pack. They were the last biplane fighters procured by the Bureau of Aeronautics, with deliveries taking place at the end of the 1930s decade. Charming as they were, the F3Fs would have fared badly against the IJN's outstanding Mitsubishi "Zero" fighters operating from the large fleet of powerful carriers. During the early years of America's involvement in WWII, aircraft of this type were serving as advanced trainers at shore stations in Texas and Florida. *USN*

Never before had any of us encountered even one in-flight Kodachrome picture of a Grumman F2F or F3F fighter from the 1930s when a trio of such slides came to hand. That occurred about the same time I obtained the remarkable Seversky SEV-3M-WW color slide, circa 1937. Here we have what appears to be the No. 2 plane from the 6th Section of VF-5 that had been in formation with two F3Fs from the 1st Section as a replacement. First Section airplanes from VF-5 would feature red on the cowlings and on the tail. The third F3F-3 has a yellow upper half cowl, but the red tail shows it was from VF-5. Fuselage designators are lost in shadow. All biplanes had the top of the upper wing painted Bright (or Chrome) Yellow. It is notable that the Grumman biplane fighters were so small that wing folding was not required (or attempted). As one example of the American aircraft production situation in 1940, Grumman Aircraft Engineering Corp. completed a plant expansion program in July, increasing floor space by a mere 32,000 sq. ft. However, early in 1941, work began on Bethpage Plant 2, adding another 480,000 sq. ft. of manufacturing area. As for the 27 Grumman F3F-3 airplanes manufactured, the last one came off the assembly line – a very loose term for the Grumman factory at that time – on 10 May 1939! The first eighteen went aboard the *"Yorkboat"* (as some called it) as replacements for Grumman F2F-1s. Wright R-1820-22 air-cooled radial engines installed provided 950 horsepower. Amazingly, Grumman proposed a replacement design in 1935, once again a biplane. The BuAer awarded a contract for the XF4F-1 on Nov. 15th 1935. Fortuitously, the Navy cancelled that contract on 10 July, 1936, replacing it with a contract for an XF4F-2 monoplane. After more major redesign, the first of 51 production F4F-3s were delivered in February 1940. That half decade was nearly disastrous for Grumman fighters.   *USN Archives*

34

For a design effort which had begun in 1935, delivery of the first production Grumman F4F-3 Wildcat was impossible before February 1940. There were no production F4F-1 or F4F-2 airplanes. The famed "Grumman Iron Works" had acted more like a lead mine in the interim. ("Ironworks" reflected an appreciation for toughness of their aircraft.) In Japan, by contrast, the Mitsubishi A6M design effort began in 1937 and the first A6M Type 0 (Zero) was ready for service in 1939. Their A6M2 Zero was faster and far more maneuverable than the Wildcat, but as we know, by 1945 the toughness of the airplane and pilot performance put the Wildcats in the winner's circle against Japanese aircraft. Each of the designs had good points and bad points, but it is well to remember in design that national psychology and many other factors tend to guide design constraints. A truly disappointing airplane in most respects was an early Wildcat contemporary, the Brewster F2A Buffalo series carrier fighters. Pudgy and unspectacular in performance, the type was second rate at best and did not serve its nation well. On the other hand, Wildcats did a yeoman job at Guadalcanal, Midway and other battles. The F4F-3 Wildcat seen here was the second production airplane (BuNo. 1845), still carrying chrome yellow paint on the upper surface of the wing. Fitted with a large prop spinner to aid engine performance and two cowl-mounted .50-cal machine guns, the airplane was being flown by test pilot S. A. Converse. The spinner and cowl guns disappeared from subsequent F4Fs and new camouflage paint schemes for naval aircraft became mandatory.   *Grumman*

In FY1935, the Curtiss Aeroplane Division of Curtiss-Wright Corp. received a contract to build what was to become the U.S. Army's first modern twin-engine attack airplane. The company had been in solid with the Army as constructor of single-engine attack and observation airplanes for a decade, but for once it did them little good. Perhaps it was not especially unusual in the 1930s for the Air Corps to express an interest in some new venture and expect a manufacturer to build a prototype as a 'Private Venture.' Curtiss, located in Buffalo, NY, designed and built their Model 76 Shrike with two new type Wright R-1670 two-row radial engines. First flown as a civil-registry airplane (X-15314) in September 1935, then tested by the Air Corps at Wright Field, outside Dayton, Ohio, it was returned to Buffalo for suggested changes. Accepted on contract in December, it was designated XA-14. A service test quantity of thirteen was procured by the AAC as the Model 76A and redesignated Y1A-18 to reflect a major engine change and use of new constant-speed propellers. The first Y1A-18 was delivered in July 1937, followed by the additional dozen in October by a hopeful Curtiss team. Probably at the suggestion of Lt. Ben Kelsey, the XA-14 was used to test a Browning 37-mm cannon installation for ultimate use in the newly ordered Lockheed XP-38 prototype. That twin-engine pursuit (think fighter), about the same size and weight as the Y1A-18s, was guaranteed to have a top speed of 400 mph, while the Curtiss could do no better than 243 mph and with far less altitude performance. It was no longer "business as usual" for the aircraft industry. Kelsey and Lockheed's young C. L. "Kelly" Johnson were about the shake the aviation world. In the meantime, Northrop Aircraft captured the bulk of Air Corps orders totaling 241 with their A-17 series single-engine attack aircraft. The Y1A-18s set a new standard, paving the way for such fine WWII airplanes as the Douglas A-20 and A-26 attack airplanes. A Curtiss A-18 Shrike displayed at Bolling Field, D.C. in January 1940 was swathed in the wash-off camouflage paint used in previous tests, but it would have been far cheaper and more practical to follow the battling British lead.   *AAC via Gerald Markgraf*

Naval Air Station Anacostia. That name rings like a ship's bell with anyone seriously interested in naval aviation. Why? Because it has a long history dating from World War I; it is located in the District of Columbia, essentially the seat of our national government; and because virtually all naval aircraft between WWI and World War II were tested at the small air station directly across the water from the War College at the juncture of the Potomac and Anacostia Rivers. When this picture was taken in the era of eight Douglas R3D Marine and Navy transports and when Kodachrome was revolutionary and new, there were only about seven naval air stations, three Marine Corps air stations, fewer than 3000 aircraft and a handful of blimps. The Naval Expansion Act authorized naval aviation to expand to 10,000 aircraft, but it would not happen overnight. Shore base expansion, stated as "one of the most pressing needs," was surging forward under a program laid down by the Hepburn Board. In contrast, the Naval Aviation Shore Establishment in August 1945 included 257 air stations and nearly 41,000 aircraft. That handful of blimps increased to 146. Prior to 1935, the Navy leased the facility from the Army, but President Roosevelt forced some air station 'horse trading' at that time. Bolling Field expanded to the south, but was immediately adjacent to the naval air station which grew greatly to meet the challenges of wartime activities.   *NHC*

Many Curtiss SBC-3s and -4s remained colorful (like this SBC-4) because they were assigned to Naval Reserve squadrons. The 1941 painting directives did not apply to reserve aircraft. Other than the specific duty station fuselage markings, the aircraft remained much the same as they had been with respect to markings applied when they flew in first-line service. These attractive biplanes had a top speed of just 237 mph (without external devices) when being delivered to the USN in February through April 1941! That is just seven mph faster than Grumman's seriously obsolete F2F-1s delivered in 1934-35. After just 35 Curtiss SBC-4s were delivered in 1940, they were put back into production in the spring of 1941. That was to more than replace the remaining earlier batch transferred to the French navy at Martinique under Lend-Lease. Brewster had failed miserably with their own XSBA-1 monoplane dive bomber, so the Navy revised it substantially and built enough for one training squadron as SBN-1s. (The XSBA-1 was slower than an F2F-1.) Against the juggernaut IJN naval aircraft, biplanes had become nothing but travesties. *USN/NA*

Even if Northrop A-17A attack airplanes were underpowered – and they were, by specification – and were particularly slow for a low-level combat mission, they were eye-catching. This fine view has an unverifiable factor. The pilot seen climbing into the aircraft is evidently a 2-star general officer. Markings on the fuselage confirmed that the photographer lacked accurate information after 60 years. The Bolling Field insignia on the fuselage confirms that this attack airplane was assigned to that Washington, D.C., Air Corps field at the time. A trio of Curtiss P-36s may be observed moving on the taxiway behind the A-17A. The location was reported to be Oklahoma. *E. W. Simpson Jr.*

For two decades, or more, before June 1941 when the Army Air Force was created, the U.S. Army ground forces wielded the power to dictate the manner in which the old Army Air Corps performed its services. In effect, it meant that attack and observation duties were of paramount importance, with tactical bombing next in line and pursuit aviation (fighters) bringing up the rear. Therefore, slavishly following the French *Armee de l'Air* concept, observation airplanes were approximately the same size and power as attack planes. The last of these large "observation" types procured in large numbers was the North American O-47 type, purchased for the Air Corps and for the National Guard. Originally designed as the General Aviation GA-15, the prototype became North American's XO-47 when the reorganized company moved to a new factory at Inglewood, California, immediately adjacent to Mines Field. This 1939 production O-47B has Wright Field Materiel Division markings. Being flown for test, only two of the normal 3-man crew appear to be aboard. Almost incredibly, the O-47B with its 1060 hp Wright Cyclone, was faster than contemporary Northrop A-17A attack airplanes. Pre-war defensive armament was minimal. North American's well-built O-47s played an insignificant role in WWII, having lost out to the more useful L (for liaison lightplanes) types and much faster photo-reconnaissance (F) planes.   *Rudy Arnold*

Grumman Aircraft Engineering Corp. struggled for design direction in 1937. Their newest naval aircraft design, the XF4F-1, still held to the biplane layout – hardly advanced from their production F3F-2 – and, even worse, estimated top speed only exceeded F3F-2 figures by about 5 percent. Revised specifications led to a radical switch to a mid-wing monoplane concept, designated XF4F-2. During simulated deck landing trials in 1938 ended in a crash. Returned to Grumman for rebuilding, it became the XF4F-3 with numerous changes. Curves of new company designs turned to angular lines and a BuAer contract for a radically different 2-engine interceptor (Design 34), epitome of the new philosophy. Angular cuts and slab panels defined the upstart XF5F-1, soon named Skyrocket. Much lighter than Lockheed's XP-38 Army pursuit, it was relatively slower and flew 14 months later – on April 1, 1940 (April Fool's Day) – than the Air Corps type. Climb speed was excellent, it had folding wings, and it was obviously designed for production. Two .50 cal. And two .30 cal. machine guns plus 40 anti-aircraft bombs in the wings was not an ideal armament mix for interception of dive and torpedo bombers. The Skyrocket had made some 70 flights prior to the delivery flight to NAS Anacostia with S. A. Converse at the controls.
Grumman

Following exhaustive tests at Bethpage, N.Y., Grumman's XF5F-1 Skyrocket was delivered – as shown – to the Navy on 22 February 1941! Two months later, the fighter was returned to the factory for changes required by the evaluation board. The towering cockpit canopy was cut down, a rather unattractive "proboscis" with square-faced shaping extended the fuselage almost to the propeller arcs, and more cooling problems had to be solved. During that period, several landing gear failures occurred, followed by a belly landing at Floyd Bennett Field at the western tip of Long Island. Ironically, the futile effort to develop the carrier-based fighter came to an end on Dec. 11, 1944, a tad over three years after the Pearl Harbor attack. An alternative development of the basic design (the G-45; later, G-46) for an AAF competition was known as the XP-50 (AC39-2517), was flown for the first time on Feb. 18, 1941, by Bob Hall. It featured revised nacelles carrying turbosuperchargers and the fuselage was fitted with a curvaceous, svelte nose with a retractable nose wheel. (A near clone of that new nose was to appear later on the very successful Grumman F7F Tigercat fighter series.) Following yet another landing gear failure, the repaired XP-50 continued on the flight test schedule, but the pursuit plane was abandoned at altitude when one supercharger turbine wheel exploded on May 14th. The pilotless plane dove into Long Island Sound. A half-decade of discouraging events was soon to end in many successes for Grumman. *Grumman History Unit*

Prior to the outbreak of war in Europe in September 1939, North American Aviation in Inglewood, Calif., had never designed or built a modern, state-of-the-art fighter airplane. But that was soon to change. On May 16, 1940, President Franklin D. Roosevelt called for Congress to pass legislation to authorize the expansion of American aircraft industry to increase production capacity to an astonishing 50,000-plane program (usually stated – incorrectly – as planes per year). In the same 10-day period, the Army Air Corps was seeking to gain approval for expansion to a legal strength of 2,700 first-line combat planes! Considering the isolationist attitude prevailing in America, the Roosevelt request was radical thinking. It turned out to be remarkable foresight. Great Britain and France had previously placed orders for training, coastal patrol and some relatively obsolescent fighter and bomber aircraft with Curtiss, North American, Douglas, Consolidated and Lockheed. Those allied nations had been instrumental in keeping the aircraft engine industry from the brink of bankruptcy. American industry responded to the call, gearing up to soon lead the Arsenal of Democracy. France, in ordering Lockheed 322-F and Curtiss H-81-A Allison-powered fighters, led the charge. But when Marshal Henri Petain signed surrender papers on 20 June 1940, the British Air Purchasing Commission took responsibility for the contracts. Those early P-40/H-81 types would be known as Tomahawks in the RAF. The Commission, under the leadership of Sir Henry Self, was aware that more production capacity was needed to produce them. Manufacturing discussions with J. H. Kindelberger and staff at North American Aviation were based on P-40 models, already obsolescent. The Curtiss XP-46 light-weight pursuit was discussed and data analyzed, ultimately rejected. Kindelberger

proposed an entirely new fighter with a newer F-series Allison engine, to be ready in 120 days. Far more producible and of new design, this NA-73X would be designed and built in 120 days!   *NAA via R. Dorr*

43

RIGHT and RIGHT BELOW Aided by the craftsmanship and detail design ingenuity of racing pilot Art Chester, the North American NA-73X prototype was a classic design from the start. Compared to the Curtiss P-40 and H-81-A Tomahawks, it was in a league of its own. Quite obviously, Lee Atwood, Edgar Schmued and Ray Rice took a page from Messerschmitt's book in creating the NA-73 design. However, they injected it with state-of-the-art features such as the NACA-sponsored/developed mid-ship tunnel radiator for Prestone cooling and the first application of the laminar-flow airfoil. According to a 60-year legend, the NAA tunnel radiator concept was borrowed from the Curtiss XP-46 "lightweight" fighter. Nonsense. At the very least, Curtiss and Republic had parallel designs featuring a tunnel radiator. The Republic concepts included the AP-10/original XP-47 (Allison engine) mockups, but contracts were awarded for two Curtiss XP-46s. At the very least, a full-scale Republic mockup was tested in the Langley-NACA wind tunnel. Considering what the RAF needs were after France fell, it is surprising that the Commission did not ask for installation of Merlin engines in the Model NA-73s. Eventually named Mustang, the fighter was ordered into production five weeks before the prototype made its first flight – bearing civil registry NX19998 – on the 26th of October. Well-known aviator Vance Breese was at the controls, as seen here, for the first eight (uneventful) test flights. Since U.S. Government approval hinged on the Air Corps receiving two production examples designated XP-51, the prototype's rudder had AAF tail stripes added for promotional reasons. A few Kodachrome photos were taken, but the watercolor striping remained on the rudder for less than four hours. On flight #9 the Allison (AC40-4395) quit with Paul Balfour at the controls, causing a forced landing. Serious damage was incurred but the NA-73X was repaired relatively soon. *NAA via R. Dorr*

LEFT Following delivery of all 77 off his Seversky P-35 pursuit aircraft and a relatively small collection of BT-8 basic trainers to the Army Air Corps in the late 1930s, the brilliant but irascible Major Alexander P. de Seversky managed to incur the wrath of most Navy and Army leaders. His actions and published writings did not endear him to government officialdom. His minor dealings with the USSR did not add to his luster. Seversky Aircraft constructed a lengthened P-35 demonstrator fighter, the EP1-68, and a 2-seater Convoy Fighter, the 2PA-BX/2PA-202, and shipped them to Europe late in November 1938 for a major sales drive. While he failed to garner orders on the Continent, the Swedish *Flygvapnet* placed significant orders for an EP1-106 version of the single-seater and for an enlarged 2PA-BX as a dive-bomber known as the 2PA-204A Guardsman. Eruption of war in Europe, an American Neutrality Act and the "Embargo action" of 10 October 1940 resulted in 60 of the fighters and 50 of the dive-bombers being confiscated by the U.S. government prior to delivery. The EP1-106s became Republic P-35As and most went to the Philippine Islands, while all but two of the 2PA-204As were redesigned AT-12 for use as trainers. In the meantime, Major Seversky had been ousted from the company, which then became Republic Aviation Corporation. Talk about sneak attacks! But that is another story. Chief tester Lowery Brabham is shown flying the first AT-12. *Republic Aviation*

RIGHT Like most of the French Government orders for first-line fighters, the purchasing effort for 91 Grumman G-36s came too late to have any impact on the Nazi assault against France and the Low Countries. Massive orders for Lockheed 322-F (Lightnings) and Curtiss H-81-A1s came far too late to have any chance of integrating them into the *Armee de l'Air*. All G-36s were to be delivered for use in the French *Aeronavale* (naval establishment) at shore facilities. Grumman flight-tested the first seven airplanes built (registered as NX-G1 through NX-G7), then delivered them as G-36As to Canada by air in conformance with the existing Neutrality Act. The temporary NX-G2 American registry reveals this as the second G-36 airplane built for France. However, all went to Great Britain's Fleet Air Arm as Grumman G-36A Martlet Is. In British service, the first two airplanes were Serial Nos. AX753 and AX754, while the following five were numbered AL231 through AL235, then flown to Montreal, Canada, in 1940. Unlike nearly all early Grumman Wildcat fighters which featured P&W R-1830 engines, the French/British Martlets were powered by single-row Wright R-1820 Cyclone engines. Out of 91 Type G-36A Martlet Is produced, ten were lost at sea. Total price was $4,318,332.00. By January 1942, Grumman was almost totally occupied with manufacturing their newer F6F Hellcat naval fighters, and Eastern Aircraft Division (GM) took over production of Wildcats and Avenger (TBM) torpedo bombers in five former East Coast automobile factories. *Grumman*

One WWII fighter that will probably be forever engraved in aviation history is the Vought F4U Corsair propeller-driven Navy/Marine fighter. Conceived early in 1938 at Stratford, Conn., the contract for a prototype XF4U-1 carrier-based fighter was received on June 11. After a prolonged, multi-year development cycle, the Corsair type went on to be one of the greatest fighters of World War II. In fact, the last Navy/Marine F4U reserve squadron decommissioned its last Corsair in June 1957. Originated as the most powerful single-engine fighter in America when first flown by Lyman Bullard on 29 May 1940, it was plagued with development problems, just as Grumman had been in the previous decade. What made the Corsair prototype so viable was its new, experimental XR-2800-4 Double Wasp engine producing a prodigious 1850 reliable horsepower. That Pratt & Whitney radial went on to become one of the best piston engines of all time. Of course it had to create a myth. Overzealous USN officialdom claimed that the prototype's unofficial speed of 405 mph on 1 October 1940 made it "the first fighter to exceed 400 mph in level flight." They conveniently failed to recall that the Lockheed XP-38 had exceeded even the 405 mph speed in February 1939. The myth lives on. Like the earlier XP-38, the XF4U-1 suffered a serious crash landing during early tests. In an accident comparable to the Lockheed prototype's accident, test pilot Boone Guyton made a forced landing on a golf course, flipping over in the 'rough' bordering the fairway. Here the XF4U-1 is seen in typical pre-war markings, including yellow paint on the wings, soon to be struck from naval requirements. *United Aircraft*

Here we have The Shape of Things to Come, and it was first flown over Baker Dry Lake in the Mohave Desert on 3 July 1940, piloted by entrepreneur test pilot, Vance Breese! This unique-design flying wing vehicle was the dream airframe of John K. Northrop who was known for his very advanced thinking. The aircraft was essentially a 45-percent scale version of the N-1 twin-engine bomber design patented by Northrop. As a flight test mock-up vehicle constructed to proof test a radical concept in flying machines, the Northrop N-1M design philosophy (seen here) was ultimately to prove more successful as an airplane than few could have believed. Even though it was seriously underpowered, it led directly to construction of two Northropz XP-56 prototype fighters and a huge long-range XB-35 experimental heavy bomber and YB-35 service test versions. Initially powered by a pair of Lycoming O-145 engines, each developing 65 hp, the N-1M – NX-2831 civil registry – barely flew. Re-engined with two Franklin 6AC-264F2, 120-hp engines, it flew extremely well. Perhaps as remarkable, at the time, was the fact that the vehicle was a variable-geometry airplane. On the ground, it was possible to vary the outer wing panel dihedral, sweepback and wingtip anhedral. Northrop's later XP-56 wartime experimental fighter drew heavily on the data accumulated by the tiny N-1M.   *Northrop via Gerald Balzer*

In the eyes of a teenager in 1940, the Northrop A-17A seemed to be the epitome of modern aircraft design. It was shiny, appeared to be constructed like a bridge, and it was colorful in prewar markings. To an aviation photo hobbyist, it was to be revered. But wait! What was really going on here? Back in 1934, Northrop submitted the XA-13 to the Air Corps for evaluation as a 6600-lb. airplane with a big Wright R-1820 engine. The last reasonably big…for the time…contract (in 1933) for attack airplanes was for the Curtiss A-12 Shrike. It amounted to 46 airplanes, the biggest award since 1930 for the category. The A-12 was essentially a 5750-pound radial-engined version of the 1932 Curtiss YA-8, proof tested with a YA-10 conversion. Northrop came back with its XA-16, essentially the earlier XA-13 airplane with a larger P&W R-1830 Twin Wasp engine. So what happened? A newer design, the 2-F led to the more efficient A-17. The AAC ordered 110 of them, but with a much less complicated landing gear and the smaller P&W R-1535 engine with 50 less horsepower. Of course the weight went up nearly another thousand pounds and the top speed dropped. A year later, they ordered another 129 newer A-17A versions with retractable landing gear, but otherwise identical to the A-17. A larger engine seemed far more appropriate, even logical, but they did boost the improved R-1535 up about 75 horsepower. In Detroit's automotive world, that was known as an annual "facelift." Recall that the contemporary NAA O-47A *observation* airplane had about 100 more horsepower from a Wright R-1820 radial engine. We will probably never know why. In about another eighteen months, NAA AT-6 trainers were just 10 mph slower than a first-line A-17A. By 1940, a 220-mph attack aircraft was likely to suffer the same disastrous fate as the RAF's Fairey Battle light bombers did during the Battle of France. *Rudy Arnold*

BELOW   One of the greatest contributions of the Arsenal of Democracy and, of course, the resulting military and naval organizations to deploy and employ the weapons was the training of military and civilian workers. Rather typical is this naval technician working on one of those hardy Grumman Ducks, in this case probably a J2F-3 of Utility Squadron VJ-4. The only partially visible marking on this temporarily lame Duck is the Neutrality Patrol national insignia above the sailor'' head. That national star was applied to carrier aircraft operating solely in the Atlantic Ocean area from 19 March 1940, modifying a directive issued in December 1939. This airplane (unconfirmed) was logically assigned to the USS *Ranger*, and from October 1940 it would probably have had a fin painted Willow Green. USN aircraft were an aviation photographer's dream come true for brilliant plumage. Carrier-based utility planes also bore blue, white, red vertical tail striping.

By February 1941, low-visibility paint schemes were applied to sea-duty aircraft and the Neutrality Patrol paint schemes began to disappear. Paint suppliers must have beenworking overtime from then on. Believe it or not,Columbia Aircraft was still producing the long-timefavorite biplane Ducks – by then J2F-6s – until mid October 1945. That was incredible longevity for a design that appeared as the Grumman XJF-1 (BuNo. 9218) for its first flight on 24 April 1933! At least a few were still flying at the turn of the century. *USN/NA*

ABOVE America was the first nation to produce and successfully fly a hydroaeroplane flying boat, a Curtiss Model F design built at Hammonsport, NY, in 1912. This country let that valuable lead slip away to other nations in World War I. Glenn Curtiss did build a reasonably successful multi-engine flying boat in 1914. Commissioned by wealthy storeowner Rodman Wanamaker, the Model H Curtiss *America* was built in an attempt to fly across the Atlantic Ocean to win a major prize of £10,000 (approximately $50,000 at the time). They created what was certainly the first successful water-based aircraft of the large flying boat type to fly. It made many test flights in he summer of 1914. The design led directly to an entire series of British flying boats during WWI. Curtiss also flew the first amphibian hydroaeroplane and then the first amphibian flying boat. Navies around the world built fleets of flying boats during the inter-war years because so much of the earth's surface is covered by lake and ocean waters. Amphibious flying boats were built in smaller numbers, but America and Great Britain produced most of the successful types. Here, a USN crew appears to be changing spark plugs on one of several Sikorsky JRS-1 twin-engine amphibians assigned to Navy utility transport duties in 1940. The lack of specialized support equipment certainly added an element of danger from falls.   *USN/NA*

In flight, taxiing on water and on beaching gear they looked enormous. That reference is being made to the Consolidated P2Y USN patrol flying boats and the civilian version called the Consolidated Commodore built for Pan American Airways. But at rest on the water, with aircrew or airplane handlers walking atop the fuselage, the flying boat (like this P2Y-2) appeared to be much smaller. Evidently a Consolidated Aircraft design in the late 1920s, it was first produced as a Martin P3M-1 when Martin underbid the Buffalo, NY, manufacturer. Consolidated fought back with an improved P2Y-1 sesquiplane version that served well in VP-5F and VP-10F as patrol flying boats in 1933 and long afterwards. Improved models known as P2Y-2s and –3s, served with VP-18, VP-19 and (in 1940) with VP-52 on Neutrality Patrol duty. Nearly all eventually found their way to NAS Pensacola, Florida, where most, if not all, aviation pilots and naval aviators logged flying time on the "P" boats. These long-range patrol planes displayed a forest of struts that could pass for telephone poles supporting a 100-ft. parasol wing. *E.W. Simpson, Jr.*

Under an umbrella of struts that resemble a tangled forest of trees, three recently commissioned naval aviators commemorate their good fortune by having the event recorded on color film in 1941. From left to right, we have Ensigns Edward Simpson Jr., Ernie Simpson and Keith Winstrom who was later to be KIA. Almost in the shadow of those 100 feet of the parasol wing on the Consolidated P2Y-2 (perhaps the one each of them had piloted as part of their Pensacola training syllabus), they knew that great adventure was ahead. Evidently all cadets of that era had to spend some time manipulating the controls of one of the P2Y series patrol flying boats that had served the country through most of the Great Depression years. When early series P2Y-1s joined patrol squadron VP-10F in 1933, they soon proved their mettle by breaking three official records. Six of them flew in formation, nonstop from San Francisco to Hawaii on January 10-11, 1934, an unprecedented event. The first-line service tail markings on these patrol flying boats had been retained. Two parallel horizontal bands on the vertical tails were indicative of Patrol Wing 4 aircraft. Total maximum horsepower available on a P2Y-1 had been 1,150 hp. These later P2Y-2s boasted 1,400 hp.   *E. W. Simpson Jr.*

On November 26, 1938, as the situation in Europe worsened, Major Seversky, his wife and test pilot George Burrell (plus service engineer Hopla) sailed for Europe with a new Seversky EP1-68 fighter and an equally new 2PA-BX two-seat fighter-bomber. It was the Major's intention to sell versions of the two airplanes to two major powers and perhaps to five other governments. The two prototype demonstrators were virtually ignored by French officials, perhaps because both Severskys would have outperformed their own Morane-Saulnier M.S.405 first-line fighters. Also, the French *Armee de l'Air* was expecting arrival of the first Curtiss H75-A in that same month (December), therefore feeling no urgent need for any Seversky types with similar performance. Swedish officials were happy to obtain such aircraft for their *Flygvapnet,* ultimately ordering 120 upgraded EP1-106 four-gun fighters and more than 52 of an enlarged 2PA-204A version of the 2PA-BX for dive-bomber service.Unlike their allies, the British showed interest in the Seversky planes when they appeared in England in March 1939. The Major demonstrated the EP1-68 at Southampton while the 2PA-BX was left with the Air Ministry for their own flight test evaluation. Later, on 1 April, Seversky flew the 2PA-BX into some bad English weather at Croydon Aerodrome. Landing at the unfamiliar airfield in heavy fog, he overran the runway and smashed into an iron fence. It could no longer be demonstrated without factory repair. Burrell demonstrated the EP1 fighter in Poland, at least, but time was running out. War clouds were everywhere.This extremely rare color photo of a production Republic EP1-106 in *Flygvapnet* service is shown for the first time. Flygvapnet *via Stridsberg*

Another *Flygvapnet* Republic EP1-106, with different markings and camouflage schemes was photographed over clouds against a clear blue sky. How did the airplane names change from Seversky to Republic, seemingly almost surreptitiously while the Major was in Europe? Seversky himself was really a poor money manager, so the financial backer – Mr. Moore – brought in Wallace Kellett, essentially under pressure from the Army and the Navy. Kellett was, realistically, a 'hatchet man." He undercut the Major in several ways while the man was busy selling aircraft in Europe. Essentially, the company was bankrupt without Moore's money, so all assets went to a new Republic Aviation Corporation, headed by Kellett. Upon his return, Seversky sued and a court battle finally settled the affair. Republic was given contracts for numerous P-43 fighters, largely based on the Major's pet project, the Seversky AP-4 with turbosupercharger in the aft fuselage. Many of his earlier AP-2 and other features were in that design. Kellett made extravagant claims about production, few of which had any merit at all. Republic proffered a P-44 design which had performance but little range.Air Corps specifications, created at Wright Field, Ohio, led to the new corporation designing the XP-47B. It was not designed in-house before Wright Field created the specifications The XP-44 never went beyond mockup stage. Evidently the EP1-106 airplanes served in the Swedish military forces for many years.   Flygvapnet *via Stridsberg*

RIGHT   On a bitterly cold morning, 11 February 1939, young Lieut. Benjamin Kelsey lifted the over-laden Lockheed XP-38 from a runway at March Field, California, in desert country south of San Bernardino. With half the wing area of a Martin B-10 heavy bomber, the experimental prototype fighter weighed within a couple of hundred pounds of a loaded B-10. Kelsey, the Fighter Projects Officer at Wright Field, was delivering the sleek silver streak to the Air Corps. With little planning or preparation, he was to refuel twice on the way to Mitchel Field, Long Island, NY, having received the blessings of Maj.Gen. H. H. Arnold, newly appointed Chief of the Army Air Corps for make an attempt on the transcontinental West to East speed record held by Howard Hughes. Very inefficient refueling stops and worse communications combined with probable carburetor icing during a traffic-prolonged landing approach to result in a crash landing. Within a few months, thirteen new service test YP-38s were ordered by Arnold, based on Kelsey's enthusiasm for the plane. The original XP-38 was designed without ideas of mass production, and it took a long time to build one example. In the event, nobody expected orders for more than 100 airplanes, so production started in a facility known as the G.G.G. Distillery across a major highway (for the time) from Union Air Terminal. It was nearly three miles from the main factory. Soon, conditions in 1940 resulted in production moving into a new major production line paralleling a Model 322-B Lightning line. Chief tester Marshall Headle took off in a YP-38 for the first time on September 18, 1940, as the Battle of Britain raged over England.   NASM

LEFT   Bell Aircraft, born of the Great Depression in October 1935, came into being only because some key Consolidated Aircraft personnel defected when the flying boat manufacturer moved to San Diego, California. Chief Engineer Robert Woods designed some spectacularly radical aircraft to meet Army Air Corps requirements. The Buffalo, NY, company's multi-seat XFM-1 escort fighter – the Airacuda – looked sleek and well armed. Bell soon followed with the radical XP-39 single-place pursuit aircraft. It was far removed from conventional-design fighter of the period and quickly garnered Air Corps and Royal Air Force orders for mass production. Overly enthusiastic performance promises soon led to British disenchantment. Quickly outclassed by standard *Luftwaffe* fighters in early operations – like the British Westland Whirlwind was – Bell Airacobra Is were soon withdrawn from European combat. RAF Orders for hundreds were cancelled, but airplane-starved Russian and USAAF commands were glad to get the new rejects. The camouflage-painted P-39C being warmed up in the New York winter contrasts with the earlier unpainted YP-39 as test pilots discuss daily flight test plans. Only thirteen YP-39s were produced in 1940, but with new facilities added production rose to 926 Airacobras in 1941. Output was more than doubled in 1942. Total production, ended in August 1944, was 9586 airplanes including the XP-39 according to Department of Commerce official records.   *Bell Aircraft*

"A day late and a dollar short" certainly applied to the French government's purchasing efforts in mid June 1940. The Anglo-French Purchasing Commission commitment for procurement of supplies and equipment from America totaled a whopping,inconceivable $1,600,000,000.00. with more than half of that committed by France. More than one billion dollars of that amount was for procurement of aircraft and engines. That was the "hot start" needed for America's defense industry, as it was called. Meantime, flying out of Wright or Patterson Field for accelerated service testing, 40-year-old Maj. Signa Gilkey was aboard one of the YP-38s (see photo) delivered from Burbank for Air Corps – there was no AAF until June 1941– testing. Diving from 35,000 feet, Gilkey was the first man to encounter "compressibility tuck" (a new phenomenon). With no knowledge of such a matter, he insisted the YP-38 suffered from tail flutter. Lockheed and Kelly Johnson's team were suddenly launched on a program aimed at solving the problem, but Kelly knew tail flutter was not involved. The tail buffeting – not flutter in any way – involved a strenuous flight test program using at least one British 322-B Lightning I and an early series P-38. Even test pilot Vance Breese was contracted to do some dive testing. (Tony LeVier had not even been hired by Lockheed yet, and had never flown a P-38.) The answer was found in wing leading edge fillets. Test item X-15 did the necessary job to correct tail buffeting. Compressibility tuck was another matter. It took a lot of company and NACA testing before a solution was found in the installation of "dive flaps." (They were never *dive brakes*.)   *NASM*

Politics and Army-Navy inter-service rivalry were rife in the second half of the 1930's decade. In that atmosphere, the tide turned illogically against the need for very long-range bombers (VLRBs), Congress imposed irrational limits on procurement of Boeing's fine B-17 type and authorized purchase of many Douglas B-18 twin-engine bombers. In March 1937, North American Aviation offered a portly, large-winged NA-21 bomber (designated XB-21) design priced-tagged at more than $122,500 each for 50 examples. It barely outperformed the existing B-18s, and Douglas retaliated with their improved B-18A, priced at only $63,977 each, exactly half of the XB-21 unit price. An Air Corps Invitation-to-Bid for twin-engine attack planes resulted in a 3-place North American NA-40 design with tricycle landing gear and a similarly equipped Douglas 7B. This duo of four planes competing met similar fates – destructive crashes. No contracts were awarded to either of the other two competitors. Douglas then developed an improved design, the DB-7. France ordered 105 of the modern high-speed attack planes. A more powerful version was ordered by the AAC in 1939 as the Douglas A-20. NAA preferred to respond to a January 1939 competition for a medium bomber, Model NA-62, having a family resemblance to the NA-40. With nearly identical wing area, the airplane was several thousand pounds heavier (loaded). Martin B-26s were ordered in quantity on August 10, 1939, with a slightly lower number of B-25s were ordered on the same day. In 1939 dollars, the Air Corps was to receive 385 medium bombers for $27,586,000.00. Only 24 of the straight B-25s were delivered, followed by forty B-25As in the configuration shown here and 118 B-25Bs because of contract revisions.   *NAA*

RIGHT Some little known facts about enclosed turbosupercharger installations only came to light about 1938 as a result of studies at the Air Corps' Wright Field Materiel Division. Previously, exposed supercharger system components seriously impeded use on pursuit (cum fighter) aircraft because of aerodynamic drag. The first enclosed system designs appeared on the belly of the Curtiss XP-37, and Lockheed's XP-38 appeared with its top-mounted installation in 1938. Soon, Bell Aircraft followed with the XP-39 arrangement closely emulating that in the XP/YP-37 situation. The famed Republic P-47 came on stage via a virtually irrelative route just two shopping days before Christmas in 1938 when Frank Sinclair made the first flight of the private-venture Seversky AP-4. In that situation, the supercharger was mounted in the bottom of the aft fuselage! No such installation had ever even been proposed for any pursuit airplane, but this was Major Alexander de Seversky's own conception, initiated as Project 65. The AP-4 was entered in the 1939 AAC High-altitude Pursuit plane competition against the Seversky XP-41 – ordered by the military – and Curtiss XP-40. Although Curtiss won the contract award –

primarily on price and G.E.'s almost invisible supercharger production rate – the XP-40 did not even meet the altitude requirements. The AP-4 (NX2597) was destroyed in a subsequent crash, but its altitude performance could hardly be ignored. Result: The Air Corps generated a contract for thirteen AP-4 Service Test airplanes equipped with G.E. Type B-2 turbosuperchargers on 12 May 1939! With the politically motivated expulsion of the Major and corporation re-designation as Republic Aviation, they became YP-43s. One of these "Baby Thunderbolts" is shown here in flight in 1940. *Rudy Arnold*

LEFT Major financier Paul Moore appointed Wallace Kellett Managing Director of Seversky Aircraft in the autumn of 1938 in Major de Seversky's absence. It did not seem to matter at Farmingdale that the founder of the company was in Europe working very hard to sell airplanes or that he ultimately succeeded. He was ousted from the company. Of course this all led, ultimately, to a significant lawsuit, but we presume the lawyers got rich, the Major got acceptable money, and Republic Aviation Corporation stockholders – primarily Moore – footed the bills. Kellett provided the press with erroneous statistics about production and orders, but few people took notice. General Arnold wanted to keep Republic's facilities and work force active, so production Lancer orders ensured that would happen. In fact, a total of 272 Lancers were delivered, the last one flown away in April 1942. Initial deliveries of the first RP-47B occurred almost immediately after the last P-43A-1-RE was delivered. More than 150 of the Lancers were converted into P-43C, D and E photographic reconnaissance airplanes, operating primarily in the CBI Theater of Operations. These Republic fighters were almost as fast as the Curtiss P-40Ns and could fight at much higher altitude. America's Flying Tigers in Asia respected the flying capabilities and altitude performance of the P-43 airplanes and would like to have had more of them. AAF armorers are shown servicing the .50-cal. fuselage machine guns and two .30-cal. wing guns. *Via Gerry Markgraf*

The old Army Air Corps was changing rapidly, its lengthy starvation diet ended with the fall of France and the Battle of Britain – and the AAC was upgraded to Army Air Forces status in June 1941. Suddenly, aviation schools were running ads in key magazines in mixed company with manufacturers like Curtiss Propeller Division. Non-aviation firms like The Austin Co. ran ads in aviation magazines, touting rapid construction of new aircraft and engine factories. Austin engineered and built huge new aircraft, engine and weapons plants for rapidly expanding manufacturers. On Long Island, for example, one 450,000-sq. ft. so-called "Blackout" plant went from first drawings to completion in 120 days. Windowless and air-conditioned, the structures revolutionized the appearance and performance of industry. The "aviation sector" of the Arsenal of Democracy was expanding under force-feeding at astounding rates. Curtiss Propeller Division followed a lead by Hamilton-Standard Propeller in resorting to new color advertising like this. Four modern Air Corps pursuit planes featuring Curtiss Electric propellers posed for ad photographs. The formation included a Republic YP-43, Curtiss P-40, Bell P-39C and Lockheed YP-38 from Wright Field, Ohio. Such ads were morale boosters for the public, not intended to sell propellers. Suddenly, photographers Rudy Arnold and Hans Groenhoff were in great demand for their pioneering color photography. Aviation pilot, mechanic and fabricator schools were converting farmers into technicians almost overnight. Document copies were spewed out rapidly by Mimeograph and blueprint machines, reproduction devices with which every man and woman in the military services and industry quickly became familiar. It was a remarkably exciting period when the initials OPM (the Office of Production Management) became as well known as GM. Soon, OPM gave way to the WPB (War Production Board) commanded by Lt. Gen. William Knudsen. The job: Create a war-based manufacturing machine to help every Allied nation defeat the Axis aggressors. *Rudy Arnold*

This may seem like a terribly harsh indictment of the Curtiss-Wright Corporation performance in WWII, but there is definitely a "Smoking Gun" syndrome readily apparent. If a direct comparison was to be made between North American Aviation's design for producibility and that involved in all Curtiss airplanes, they were at opposite poles. The P-40 series was "ancient" compared to the NAA P-51 or the Messerschmitt Bf.109Fs. It took far too long and far too many redesigns to make the SB2C dive-bombers combat worthy. Curtiss SO3C Seamew airplanes were blatant warfare failures. Out in St. Louis Division, they tried to manufacture wooden C-76 Caravan freighters, with plans to produce others at Louisville, KY, and one other Curtiss subcontractor. Just think of the WPB's infinite wisdom. Three sources for simple wooden transports, but only one major production source for complex P-38s!

Some early examples of the C-76 literally fell apart. All orders were cancelled, not just because the aluminum shortage was quickly overcome, but because of the ultimate failure of the C-76 Caravan. A Curtiss XF14C-2 Navy fighter went no place. Late in the war, the XBTC-2 naval torpedo bomber also did not meet the challenge. Much-needed Curtiss SB2C dive-bombers took years to get into service, despite being a pre-war design. Accidents of the nature shown in the two XSB2C-1 "hard landing" pictures should not have happened. Well-designed aircraft do not normally break in half, especially those designed for aircraft carrier operations. After the end of hostilities, the renamed Curtiss Airplane Division ceased to be a significant contributor to the American aviation scene. *Jack Kerr via W. Thompson*

Douglas Aircraft Co. has had a decades-long record of manufacturing excellent airplanes, but the record was imperfect. There can be little doubt that among the best were the DWC World Cruisers, DC-3s/C-47s, A-20s and, of course, the C-54/DC-4 transports. However, their B-18 and B-23 designs were well behind the state-of-the-art curve. Had the B-23 seen here been able to appear two years earlier to garner orders placed for the B-18As, it might have been a decent factor in WWII. Numerous authors have presumed that the B-23 initially was in contention for contracts garnered by the Martin B-26 and North American B-25 entries, but it was really a "stopgap" bomber pending issuance of the then radical specification that called for a 350 mph medium bomber. In actual fact, the first of 33 flew on 27 July 1939, while the Glenn Martin Co. competition-winning design proposal did not reach an Army evaluation board until 5 July 1939. Ultimately, the Douglas B-23 design fell far short of all existing requirements and they served only in coastal patrol and high-speed transport roles in WWII. A departing senior staff officer is seen shaking hands with a base officer prior to boarding. *E. W. Simpson Jr.*

LEFT & BELOW: Most people are unaware that the famed Consolidated B-24 and C-87 family of WWII bombers and transports were fraternal twins following a commercial flying boat sibling. In fact, seeing the prototype XB-24 in silhouette, one could easily have presumed it was the Model 31 flying boat in flight. With absolute certainty, we know that the high-aspect-ratio Davis wing seen on all B-24s and C-87s was the starting point for Model 32 bombers, quickly known as the B-24. The tail design, deep fuselage (hull) – similar in profile, at least – plus the wing planform and airfoil were far more than passively close in design. Even the bomber's nose profile imitated a flying boat hull shape. The greatest differences were in substitution of four Pratt & Whitney radial engines for the two Wright Double Cyclones that powered the Model 31 flying boat, and the use of a retractable tricycle landing gear on the bomber. The B-24 series was surely the first four-engine bomber type in the world to employ a tricycle landing gear. In fact, all three Air Corps bomber designs of that period (B-24, B-25 and B-26) put into production in America in that 1940 time frame featured tricycle landing gears. When the XB-24 came into being, the French Purchasing Mission jumped on the bandwagon soon after the bomber flew for the first time, two days before New Year's eve, 1939, placing an order for 120 examples. Recalling that this was the time of the so-called "Phony War" prevailing on the Continent, France was desperately hoping to obtain a fleet of long-range bombers out of an undeveloped prototype. What was needed in 1939 was not 4-engine bombers; what they needed was more time and they squandered it by declaring war against an armed Germany. Certainly, in due time, the *Wehrmacht* would have turned westward and attacked, but America needed time to build its arsenal plus time to develop the needed weapons. France had frittered away its No. 1 position as an airpower in the mid Thirties, while the U.S.A. struggled with the economy and was handcuffed by a desire to be isolationist while also flirting with Communism as a panacea for the Depression. Like it or not, the World's salvation from the forces of tyranny gaining strength in dictatorships existed in only one place. That was in American industry, the youngest nation of them all. The USAAC and RAF Consolidated LB-30A Liberator I transports (shown here) were undeveloped prototypes for bombing duties, incapable of serving successfully in that combat role. Like non-combat troops, they served their operators well in transporting critical personnel and supplies over great distances of land and water. More importantly, they led the way to production of no fewer than a total of 18,188 Liberators delivered to the AAF and the USN. Additionally, 1,694 Liberators were supplied directly to the RAF from Consolidated. Ford's Willow Run Bomber plant produced no fewer than 6,791 bombers, beginning in 1942[3]. *Via Robert D. Archer*

[3]The author, having been rejected for pilot training (eyesight), was employed as a structural repair designer at Willow Run in July 1942. In final assembly, the first handful of B-24Es was moving toward flight test and delivery. Early in March 1943, he joined the USAAF, serving for the most part in the HQ ATC Flight Test Unit until 1946.

Suddenly Last Summer.....From the motion picture of the same name. It was June, 1941, in sunny California. The rapidly growing Arsenal of Democracy had received a real shot in the arm with passage of the Lend-Lease Act by Congress in March. President Roosevelt was empowered to lend "defense articles" to any nation whose defense was considered vital to the safety of the United States of America. No longer was it necessary for Britain to buy on a "cash-and-carry" basis. Lockheed-Vega, in Burbank, California, was expanding production at a remarkable rate. While YP-38s were being tested, Army Air Corps P-38Ds and RAF 322-B Lightnings were being built inside the factory buildings and outside. Into this maelstrom of activity drifted an old wooden antique, built in January 1933. Originally bought by Continental Oil Company of Oklahoma, and still owned and flown by "Conoco" of Colorado, it had arrived on a special-need mission. This Lockheed Vega 5C Special, c/n 194, needed a major overhaul and engine to test a propeller anti-icing device. The old, well-used cabin monoplane was deemed ideal for the job. Some old-timer Lockheed employees from the early 1930s were made available for the job. Here we see NC12282 in Lockheed's "outback" in its first stages of rework, sorely needed.
Lockheed

Painted, primped and polished, the old workhorse Lockheed Vega 5C Special was evidently rolled out of new Building 146 at Lockheed Plant B-1. In a matter of hours, it was to acquire the large anti-icing spinner for test purposes. Although the CAA issued a change in license number to NR12282, it is evident that no such change appeared on the airplane as long as it was in Burbank. In fact the NC version was outlined in white to make it more legible. By way of explanation about the name of Vega Aircraft Corp., the business was created in 1937 under the name of AiRover as a Lockheed affiliate. By 1938, the name was changed to Vega Airplane Co. in honor of the famous Lockheed Vega (as seen here), all necessary for business reasons. Vega Aircraft produced a military derivative of Lockheed's Lodestar airliner, naming it the Ventura. It was a high-performance outgrowth of the Hudson series, sold to Great Britain in large numbers. The U.S. Navy and AAF acquired significant quantities of Vega Ventura and Harpoon patrol bombers under designations PV-1 and PV-2 for USN, B-34 and B-37 for the new USAAF. The Conoco Vega 5C served the oil company well throughout the war, being sold as the Allies neared victory against Germany, Italy and Japan. Heavy snow loading in 1954 broke the Vega's back and it was scrapped in March.To the right is one of the first YP-38 Lightnings.   *Lockheed*

Cruising serenely, resplendent in its prewar plumage, this United States Coast Guard Lockheed R5O-1 executive transport (V188) portrayed a picture of peace. This was a one-of-a-kind aircraft in the USCG service, carrying a Navy model designation before Pearl Harbor was attacked; it was in every respect a Lockheed Model 18 Lodestar airliner. Essentially, it was employed to transport top executive officers and VIPs from the Treasury Department. The sleek R5O-1 was delivered on 14 May 1940, having cost the then princely sum of $185,000.00. During the subsequent war years under Navy jurisdiction, the USCG operated three R5O-4 and four R5O-5 Lodestars in service, most likely having been transferred from USN lists. Use of Bureau of Aeronautics designations before the Coast Guard actually came under Navy control in World War II stemmed from procurement through Navy contracts. This airplane bore the designation R5O-1 (the letter O signifying Lockheed). That type proved to be the forerunner of the Vega Ventura reconnaissance-bomber developed under a British contract. Vega delivered Ventura bombers – derived directly from the Lockheed Lodestar – to the Royal Air Force; then to the AAF as B-34s and B-37s; also to the U.S. Navy as PV-1s (the letter V signifying Vega). But later in the war, PV-2 Harpoons were known as Lockheeds. All very confusing. It had to do with technicalities of Lockheed absorbing the subsidiary Vega as a division during the course of the war. *USCG*

One of the great mysteries of life surrounds the total British failure to explain with honesty their absolute rejection of the Lockheed 322-B Lightning I aircraft when there was still a dire need for fighters, especially long-range fighters. From what we know, most of the cause can be traced to the RAF local representative at Burbank after testing the first airplane for acceptance. Little if anything, of evidentiary value has been divulged in documented case history evidence in any British or other journal. Hardly a handful of the type was actually accepted in any form before the Air Ministry cancelled the entire order. Off course the entire French order for 322-F airplanes was initially taken over by Great Britain in the summer of 1940. The RAF absolutely knew that the airplanes were to be minus turbosuper-charging and with both propellers turning in the same direction – courtesy of the *Armee de l'Air* specifications. It would have been logical for the Air Ministry to accept a small percentage of Lightning Is, but opting for supercharged Lightning II equivalents of the P-38E by means of change orders. As a result, Lockheed's Robert Gross was forced to bring a lawsuit against our English cousins. Why in the world didn't Air Ministry "boffins" propose installing Rolls-Royce or Packard Merlins in place of the Allison C-series engines? At a much later date, Rolls-Royce engineers did just that with a few Allison-powered Mustangs, but surely somebody could have suggested conversion of the Lightning Is in 1940. Perhaps the English minds were not well acquainted with American hot-rodding of cars at the time, a practice that can change the entire character of any vehicle, be it waterborne, airborne or on terra firma. Such eccentricities in people boggle the mind. More than a half century later, the smooth lines and shapeliness of the Lighting I pleasures the senses. This 322-B is seen over the Southern California coastline. *Eric Miller-LAC*

64

Chapter 2

A Day of Infamy - Then, Unleashing the Arsenal

WAR! Suddenly, on a normal, quiet Sunday in the continental United States of America, far removed from that December 7, 1941, scene of infamy centered on Pearl Harbor, in Hawaii, the life of virtually every American was changed forever. The news came to each of us, at various times, by radio or telephone. Or perhaps it came from some neighbor running up and down the street yelling about the cowardly attack on our great naval installation at beautiful Hawaii. No bombs fell on the Continental United States, probably mitigating the fury to an extent. The ranting of the Isolationists ceased almost instantly, but not without some of them insisting it was a hoax attributable to the president. Suddenly, however, being an "America First" party member was not considered to be patriotism at its best. In fact, at least for a time, America's aviation hero, Charles Lindbergh, was badly tarnished since he had been a public voice for them. Unhorsed, he ultimately rose to the challenge, realized his stubbornness had served him badly, and then moved on to do all possible to aid his fellow Americans and allies. In that, he was successful.

To the majority of Americans, the Pearl Harbor attack seemed to be incomprehensible, especially when the culprits were a people we had little but contempt for. How they had the temerity, the audacity to even think of such a thing was beyond understanding. Eventually thoughts turned to the question: Who was responsible for allowing this attack on America and the Philippine Islands to happen? In those days, most Americans could have looked in the mirror to see one of those culprits. However, they too, for the most part, rose to the challenge. As might be expected, later evidence pointed to Flag-level commanders in charge at Hawaii, but rarely if ever at some insignificant military and naval personnel who failed in every way to use logic in performing there sworn duties. And, of course, it was unthinkable that those top-ranking officers and civilians in Washington should ever be allocated a proper share of the blame. Most certainly, people at the very top in the War and Navy Departments, if not the State Department – as any thorough study of the evidence will reveal – were culpable if not totally to blame. They, of course, escaped unharmed. The smoking guns, if not the actual bullets,

were evident. Politics and public morale will always take precedence over truth.

It did not take long for reality to set in. Though hidden for a time – perhaps a very long time – the shortcomings in many areas of our leadership took their toll. Hawaii was – sad to say – wide open to any coordinated invasion. Had the Imperial Japanese Army and Navy been prepared to the level that had existed in planning instead of ignoring the requirements of their original plans, the islands would most certainly have fallen just as did the Philippine Islands. America would have made just as many unforgivable mistakes, something that cannot seem to be avoided by human beings. Appropriate evidence: Given the actions of the Nazi war machine and the failures incurred by the French, Belgians, Dutch, British (in Europe and Asia), more than a decade of Japanese aggression in Asia, and even Russian aggression against Finland, how could America's military, naval and civilian leaders be completely surprised by Japanese actions? Voices raised in warning by many observers were the subject of high-level ridicule. Given any understanding of Japanese aims in the Far East and their needs for survival – man's greatest natural instinct – not even to mention the scope of their military and naval buildup plus their alliance with the Axis, Americans proved to be asleep at the switch. In their own way, many responsible men were as corrupt as were the Quislings in Norway.

M/Gen. Frank M. Andrews, chief of our Air Corps fighting arm, spoke up in January 1939 in an honest effort to awaken the nation to the fact that the U.S. was a fifth- or sixth-rate air power in the world. By February, he was replaced by a Brigadier General. Andrews was demoted to a lower-level job for having attempted to alert Americans to the sorry state of our Air Corps. Sixteen long months later, President Roosevelt, speaking before Congress, asked them to pass legislation aimed at facilitating expansion of the aircraft industry to produce no less than the unheard of rate of 50,000 airplanes a year. It was like a bolt from the blue.

When reality did creep in, like the actions that always follow the evidence of a heart attack, the "Sleeping Giant" had already found two giant allies in being that would permit us to overcome the Axis war machine. First, and most important was the Arsenal of Democracy that had been created by two entities: Foreign orders showered on our industrial and natural resource giants, and the creation of the Military Draft. At a fairly early date, the Office of Production Management (OPM) had to be created to control our elaborate industrial resources. Congress had, reluctantly, approved and funded the military draft, and bodies were soon in uniform for at least initial military training. Close on the heels of congressional approval of declarations of war against the Axis nations, the OPM – which had really done a good job of expanding all facets of our manufacturing and transportation infrastructures – was reorganized (logically) as the War Production Board (WPB). America's industrial might was already up and running. It would expand to levels unlikely ever to be seen again, something that the Japanese and Germans had both underestimated. Perhaps even the Isolationists had served some good purpose in convincing the Japanese and Germans that this nation had no real will to fight.

In the early stages of the United States' participation in warfare, the government agencies also deluded Americans with watered-down, inaccurate reports of our losses and defeats on the battlefronts of the world. Of course that was intended to keep morale up, but an informal press corps and radio news managed to assist in bringing out the best in a unified population. Until such realities became widely evident, many Americans believed, with sincerity, that we could defeat any enemy with one hand tied behind the back. Those in military service became realists long before the general public got the message. We had tough enemies to fight, and the cost would exceed even the wildest estimates made by pre-war realists.

Some considerable time later, the "Pogo" comic-strip character created by Walt Kelly was right on target when a quote attributed to him appeared in the newspaper comic strips. Pogo stated rather succinctly and accurately that, "We have met the enemy and he is us." That statement could logically have related to the situation existing in the United States in the first two years of the 1940s decade. We can never seem to learn that aggressors operate from a position of strength and surprise. And you only give them more reasons for being aggressive by making idle threats aimed at deterring them when they recognize your extreme weaknesses stemming from their knowledge that your population is disunited. That is exactly what occurred in the weeks before the Japanese attack. Our leaders – military, political and diplomatic – showed evidence of being on different wavelengths. Strong evidence exists to show that a dictatorial General George Catlett Marshall arrogantly refused to accept warnings from informed but lower-level Intelligence personnel and strategists. Marshall revealed an unwillingness to even discuss such matters with his staff and advisors. Accordingly, he failed to provide his subordinates in Hawaii with strong messages or direct orders that should have alerted them to the extreme gravity of the situations as they really existed. As it turned out, General Short and Admiral Kimmel were not alerted to much, if any, of the political and diplomatic conditions at the hub in Washington, D.C., so in typical military/naval parlance nobody at the top levels took the subsequent "heat." That situation has existed for many, many decades. Rarely – as a later president was to say – did the "buck stop here."

Marshall is remembered for his gratuitous treatment of defeated enemies at war's end, but his detachment from conditions in 1941 has rarely been recognized.

Did our leaders have any real justification in not being alerted to the evidence that aerial warfare had changed drastically from the way it was being used in the two decades following Germany's defeat in World War I? Everybody in the key rungs of the War and Navy Departments is supposedly trained to the hilt in the art of warfare.

That is thought to be their focal point in a career job. And who should have a better perspective of the war-making potential if any nation than the diplomatic corps of the State Department? Why have intelligence corps if nobody heeds their warnings? But, how can one account for the actions that America launched perhaps a year after war erupted in Europe? The Navy's Pacific Fleet was moved from headquarters on the West Coast to Hawaii in 1940 for no other reason than the knowledge of Japan's expansionist aims in the Far East. That movement to the Hawaiian Islands and the start of defensive developments on Guam, Midway and Wake Islands was unprecedented. Facility expansions in the Philippines were rushed and our best first-line fighters and bombers were sent to those Pacific bastions. Had it not been for one tough-minded general, preparations for defense in Alaska and the Aleutian Islands would have remained at Depression levels of development. Finally, in January 1940, the Army rushed to build an airbase at Anchorage; concurrently, the Navy began work on airfields at Sitka and Kodiak, also began construction of a naval base at Dutch Harbor.

While many of these massive projects became headline makers, the long peacetime mindset in the Navy and Army caused the lower echelons to totally ignore good military logic in operations and facilities. After all, the battleship navy was our first line of defense. Changing such a mindset is extremely difficult at best. If Great Britain, France, Belgium and Holland properly judged Hitler and Nazism and Mussolini and his broad aims perhaps they would have expanded their own forces accordingly. They all had plenty of time and reasons to react, especially when all of the world could see what the Germans were doing in the Spanish Civil War. The Allies would not have been desperate enough to literally throw money at American industry in a desperation move to match German and Italian military and naval expansion. In the U.S.A., our steel, aluminum and automotive industries were relatively healthy in the late 1930s, but the aircraft and engine industries were – by comparison – withering on the vine. A huge order for naval fighters was for fifty airplanes over a two-year period. Congress would only fund the purchase of the least expensive, but totally ineffective bombers so that the numbers would come closer to authorized strength. Effectiveness of the weaponry was secondary. Therefore, the flood or orders for aircraft, trucks and ships coming from Europe – beginning in 1938 – pushed those industries to expand.

The thing that makes it all very hard to understand as to why our army and navy were essentially caught flat-footed in the Pacific by a fifth-rate power, especially when there were so many warning signs prevalent. The Pacific Ocean was said to cover an expanse of 64 million square miles. Yet, a week after the Hawaiian newspapers trumpeted a clarion call of warning, every battleship of the Pacific Fleet was anchored close to Ford Island in a double line, merely feet separating bows and sterns. If they were afraid of saboteurs, why were there essentially no guard details and small patrol boats anywhere to be seen. True, there was paranoia rampant all around the islands, but was General Short and his staff so blind about the capabilities of dive bombers and torpedo planes that he lined up every first-line fighter without fuel or ammunition. The were like sitting ducks for air attack. Worse, had an actual saboteur managed to throw thermite bombs into just two aircraft at night, the entire line of fighter could have been destroyed. Logic, based on British and German experience in Europe, would scream that dispersal was mandatory. There was plenty of manpower that could have been placed on emergency guard duty, with all weekend and other leaves cancelled.

"Yellow Peril, "step aside. Such could have been the Stearman Company's comment to the NAF N3N primary trainers seen in large numbers at Pensacola and NAS Corpus Christi, Texas. The colloquialism "Yellow Peril" was applied indiscriminately to all N3Ns The N2S series was essentially a slight variation of the original Army Air Corps Stearman PT-13 and PT-15 models developed from the X-75 prototype. Kaydet primary trainers helped to raise pilot proficiency to a high standard, just having enough vices to keep a student on his toes as he learned. Many thousands of the Stearmans were manufactured in the Midwest during the war, far outnumbering the N3Ns turned out by the Naval Aircraft Factory in Pennsyl-vania when production was ended about Christmastime, 1941. A total of 816 N3Ns had been produced. This stacked echelon of N2Ss would indicate that by the time primary training was completed, pilot proficiency was quite high. As an aside, to better understand the real impact of the Great Depression on everything, there were absolutely no funds appropriated by Congress between August 1932 and June 1933! Therefore, no flying personnel were trained for at least that length of time. In fact, it was only concurrent with the commissioning of the USS *Ranger* (CV-4) on 4 June 1934 that it became evident that a new cadet program had to be implemented. *USN/R. Starinchak*

This Bell Airacobra I was quite colorful, but the painters took several liberties with the paint scheme, notably the white underside areas. It is apparently AH570, the first one assembled and flown. If the fighter was not a poor performer, it certainly was a maintenance headache to the RAF. USAAF personnel found that out during the summer military maneuvers in the southern states in 1941. All sorts of unexpected problems were encountered, the most shocking being departure of the entry doors in flight. In England, the Air Fighting Development Unit had the first encounter at operations with the new Bell. Evidently things were not so bad that the type could not be assigned to operations with 601 Squadron. Like the Westland Whirlwind and Boulton Paul Defiant fighters, the Airacobra did not even shape up in the RAF's view for duty in North Africa or Southeast Asia. Far more important in the overall history of the Airacobra is demonstrated inability to ever fly air-to-air combat missions against Messerschmitts and Focke-Wulf fighters over *Festung Europa.* Well-trained USAAF pilots, in dire circumstances, made even the P-400 re-identified version of the Airacobra I a useful tool in 1942 in the southwest and northwest Pacific arena. In this picture, the long-barrel Hispano-Suiza 20-mm cannon is not seen protruding at least a foot from the propeller spinner of the initial Airacobra I .   *Bell via G. Markgraf*

"If it looks right it must be right!" That is an age-old adage that would seem to have been appropriate for the extremely attractive Bell Model 14, seen here in the guise of the RAF's Airacobra I. Unfortunately, the seemingly very advanced fighter for its time did not live up to the ballyhoo put out by Bell Aircraft's sales people. Certainly the publicity and sales releases were made with the approval of company chief, Laurence "Larry" Bell. The Robert Woods' design was in response to a 1936 specification and it won the competition for a single-engine, high-altitude Pursuit (fighter) airplane in 1937. However, military budgets in the USA guaranteed that the Army Air Corps was not going to be on a par with the leading air powers with contemporary timing. For example, the wonderful British Supermarine Spitfire Mk. I, built to a 1934 specification, managed to attain a speed of 355 mph on 880 hp with a fixed-pitch, 2-blade wood propeller in 1937. The prototype, experimental Bell (Model 4) XP-39 did not even fly until March 1939! It also was flown about two months later than the contemporary Lockheed XP-38, a far more complex twin-engine airplane. Bell touted the XP-39 as a 400-mph fighter; according to formal NACA performance documentation, the best top speed at power-rated altitude was 327 miles per hour. Of course, ballyhoo also described the Curtiss XP-40 of that same period as a 400-mph fighter, while it actually was capable of less than 350 mph. In its initial form, the

XP-39 was equipped with a G.E. turbosupercharger, aimed at providing a fighting altitude of more than 25,000 feet. Neither the Spitfire nor the P-40 had that capability at the time, but NACA influence caused the Air Corps to delete that key item from all subsequent P-39s. That altered the entire original concept, dooming all Airacobras to second-rate status as a viable fighter. A war-panicked French Purchasing Commission ordered no fewer than 275 examples of what amounted to a P-39C (80 planes) type. While the Army Air Corps (at the time) changed most to P-39Ds featuring armor plate and self-sealing fuel tanks, there is no certainty such changes applied to the French Model 14s. With the fall of France in June 1940, the British Direct Purchase Commission, with 400 already on order, took over the obligation. Eventually enough Airacobra Is arrived in England to be assigned to RAF's 601 Squadron, replacing Hawker Hurricanes. Assigned initially to low-level strike missions, it proved deficient even in that role.   *Bell via G. Markgraf (2)*

BELOW   Hall Aluminum PH-2 and PH-3 flying boats were well suited to rescue of large numbers of persons requiring such actions at sea. These seaplanes were developed offshoots from the USN's Hall XPH-1, a metal-hulled version of earlier Naval Aircraft Factory patrol aircraft. In actual fact, the NAF XP4N-1 was nearly identical to the XPH-1 except for the powerplants and the use of twin vertical tailplanes. The biplane wings – arrangement and structure – date back to NAF designs of the PN-8 and famous PN-9 of 1925. Therefore, we have the design essentials of flying boats flown in 1925 still flying what amounted to combat missions for the Coast Guard in 1944, at the very least. One can only presume that American, British and French intelligence organizations were either operating like college fraternities or barely existed at all in the early 1930s. Sleeping Giant, indeed! Probably comatose would be more appropriate. The closest we seemed to come to an "Alert!" was reading stories in *Flying Aces* magazine. Namely the old "Buzz Benson" stories; factual fiction. As for the seven Hall PH-3s of 1939-40, at last amenities for the pilots included a nice "turret top" enclosure, providing protection from the weather. However, the gunners were still exposed to open sea, open air elements. Their greatest protection was the distance enemy fighters would have to fly to attack them. A formation of biplanes in flight, such as these three PH-3s over Florida waters in World War II has to be at least equal to seeing the launch of a Curtiss F9C-2 fighter from the ZRS-5, better known as the USS *Macon*.   *Rudy Arnold/USCG*

ABOVE   Hall Aluminum Aircraft Co. was hardly to be classed as a major contractor to the Navy, but they did manage to secure some contracts over a period of two decades. They pioneered in construction of all-metal seaplanes and flying boats. After building and testing a prototype XPH-1 for the Navy, some considerable time passed before they received a BuAer contract for nine production PH-1s in the Great Depression days. They served only in one squadron, hardly unusual in those days of very tight budget allocations. Under the Treasury Department, USCG assignments created a need for some large patrol bombers, but the Navy had priority on obtaining new Consolidated PBY airplanes. Seven modernized Hall PH-2 biplane flying boats were ordered in 1938 at a cost of $116,100 each for those duties. Evidently the PH-2s served their Coast Guard masters well until 1944. Replacement aircraft were seven new PH-3s (V177 through V183) featuring much improved flight deck accommodations, long chord NACA cowlings and 750-hp Wright Cyclone engines. Retirement of biplane flying boats from the USCG occurred not long after the war with the Japan ended. Flight in biplane flying boats in WWII was closely akin to similar experiences for crews in WWI. *Rudy Arnold via R. Starinchak*

RIGHT   We cannot imagine any Curtiss-Wright test pilot, other than Herb Fisher, having this, er, ugh, chunky build, so we presume it was he. Fisher was more likely to have been seen preparing to climb into any Curtiss P-40, especially since he is reputed to have flown every P-40 ever built….at least once, but that is most certainly an O-52 Owl behind him. At least he was dressed as any test pilot would be in winter of 1940-41 at Buffalo, NY. The photographer at Curtiss (Buffalo) remains to this day an unknown color photographer in that era, but his work demonstrates he was one of the best of the genre.   *Jack Kerr via W. Thompson*

LEFT   In a winter atmosphere in Buffalo, N.Y., during 1941 Curtiss Aeroplane Division employees work on a new Curtiss O-52 Owl observation aircraft. Pratt & Whitney's R-1340-51 Wasp single-row radial engine with a 3-blade Hamilton-Standard propeller is seen getting all the attention prior to a scheduled test flight. At this particular time, it is interesting to note that the Curtiss observation type had the same engine scheduled for use in contemporary AT-6 and SNJ training aircraft soon to be ordered by the Air Corps and the USN. Although the new O-52 had approximately 400 less horsepower than the North American O-47B, it was only about 15 mph slower, primarily because it weighed about one ton less and was a "cleaner" design. Perhaps the Army was beginning to learn some lessons from the war in Europe where the British Westland Lysander army co-operation type of roughly similar design was proving to be quite useful.   *Jack Kerr via W. Thompson*

Mechanics assigned to care for this new Curtiss O-52 posed proudly with their charge in the winter of 1940-41. In appearance, the airplane could hardly be faulted. It still is shapely, even at the time of the new millennium, some 60 years later. The "Grease Monkeys" haven't changed much in clothing style in those six decades. On the other hand, that hangar with the upward-pointed flood or spot light looks as if it could have been appropriately cast in the role of a building seen in the movies "Ceiling Zero" or "Desert Airport" (from RKO Pictures?) in the 1930s. *Jack Kerr via W. Thompson*

TOP Beauty is in the eyes of the beholder, of course, and it appears that the O-52 Owl in flight should have elicited rave reviews. The cowl lines were either borrowed from the Curtiss-Wright (St. Louis) CW-23, or at least the CW-21B, designs or perhaps evoked excitement about cowling design in that Missouri design crew. A landing gear retraction arrangement, traceable back to the 1920 Dayton-Wright RB-1 racer (or the Grumman XF2F-1), was a neat rendition of the system used on the Curtiss XF13C-1 fighter. One has to guess that the same design team that worked on that fighter at least lit the flame on the O-52 design. With the same P&W Wasp engine found in any NAA AT-6, and a 3-blade propeller, any person has to wonder why the airplane type was not produced in serious numbers as a training plane. As a photographic vehicle, it challenges the much later Cessna 190-195 radial-engined private aircraft, but the Cessna had a cantilever wing as frosting. Perhaps it was not as good as it looked, even though approximately as fast as an AT-6. The O-52 faded rapidly from view, even though it might have been priced as low as $600 as War Surplus. *Rudy Arnold*

RIGHT A camera seems to be a magnetic attraction. This Curtiss Aeroplane Division teams and either the foreman or engineer could not resist the temptation to "look at the birdie" when the camera centered on them. The tail of the aircraft raised on a portable trestle is a Navy Curtiss SBC-4 carrier-based scout bomber. When Jack Kerr took this picture, America was less than a year away from being at war with Japan and Germany, but factory workers are still working on biplane dive bombers. No, this was not one being prepared for transfer to the French Navy air arm for use on the carrier *Bearn* because all SBCs sitting on that carrier deck were rotting away. France had capitulated to Nazi Germany many months earlier. Perhaps Curtiss was completing overhaul work on this and other airplanes of the type. It seems obvious that these men are conducting a compass calibration, using the rudimentary compass rose. With larger contracts, they had to become more sophisticated. That airplane in the background happens to be a Bell P-39D, after most Cs were converted with self-sealing tanks and more armor plate and glass. *Jack Kerr via W. Thompson*

BELOW   Seattle's Boeing Aircraft Company followed great success of its P-12/ F4B AAC and Navy biplane fighter planes with the remarkable peacetime P-26 "Peashooter." They manufactured no fewer than 136 examples in the midst of what had to be the worst Depression of the Nineteenth and Twentieth Centuries. However, they "jumped the gun" in bringing their XP-/YP-29 Air Corps fighters to the fore too soon with too little to offer. An offspring, the Navy XF7B-1 monoplane had little to offer against Grumman's newer biplane fighters. Fortunately, Boeing put most of their limited 1934 resources into development of the new 4-engine bomber of advanced design, the 299-X (incorrectly XB-17). Unlike the XB-15 very-long-range development bomber program, begun earlier in the year with AAC funding, the smaller, faster Model 299 was designed and built for a "fly-off" competition – scheduled for August 1935 at Wright Field. At the time of the competition invitation received in August 1934, company employment was down to 600 or one-third of what it had been in January. The private venture 299-X was rolled out of final assembly on July 17, 1935, barely in time for testing before the need to appear in Dayton, Ohio, for the competition against the Douglas DB-1 (XB-18). A hidebound, myopic congress combined with an ultra-conservative Army Chief of Staff awarded major contracts to Douglas for a bomber that barely met the "soft" requirements. A stupid mistake by an AAC test pilot – taking off with external control locks in place – caused the plane to crash and burn. At the time, the 299 was far ahead of the competition in all performance areas, but the DB-1 was cheap, so many could be procured. In an obviously "guilt-ridden" decision, the AAC awarded a service test contract for thirteen YB-17 bombers in January 1936, all redesignated Y1B-17 by delivery time. One of the service test airplanes, cloaked in camouflage paint, is shown at Langley Field, Virginia, in the 1941-42 era.   *Library of Congress*

ABOVE   Just a few short months beyond a decade after America entered World War I in April 1917, a large aviation research and development facility was dedicated a few short miles outside of Dayton, Ohio. On October 12, 1927, Wright Field was dedicated as the home of the Materiel Division of the newly designated Army Air Corps. A little more than six years later, that organization was commissioning construction of two enormous Very Long-Range Bombers. The first was Boeing's XLRB-1, the second being Douglas' XLRB-2, later to be redesignated XB-15 and XB-19 respectively. Maximum range for the XLRB-2 was specified as 7,710 miles in 55 unrefueled flying hours. Maximum bomb load was to be 18.5 tons. Of course maximum bomb load and maximum range were not expected to be concurrent. Four Wright R-3350-5 Double Cyclone engines provided a total of 8,000 hp for the monster with its 212-foot wingspan. As the XB-19 (AC38-471), it was completed in Douglas' (Santa Monica) huge round-top assembly building at Clover Field, California. Major Stanley Umstead piloted America's largest airplane from that base for the first time on June 27, 1941. Armament was to consist of two 37-mm cannons, five .50-cal. machine guns and six .30-cal. machine guns, with one of the cannons mounted in the 360-degree revolving turret on top of the XB-19. Gross weight of the bomber was 162,000 pounds. Before the war ended, four Allison V-3420-11 twenty-four-cylinder engines, each with a displacement of 3,420 cubic inches supplanted the original Wright R-3350s. This picture was probably taken at March Field after Maj. Umstead brought it over from Santa Monica. The early model P-40 was parked under the XB-19's wing to emphasize the bomber's massiveness.   *USAAF via Walter Boyne*

Dating back to 1911 as an aircraft manufacturer, the Glenn L. Martin Co. reversed a trend by starting in California and eventually settling in at Middle River, Maryland, inn 1928. Martin B-10/B-12 bombers of the early 1930s were probably the most advanced bombing aircraft in the world with speed capability of at least 212 mph by 1934. Just six short years later, the company submitted its radically new Martin Model 179 medium bomber design to the Army Air Corps. In a design competition with two other contenders – the North American NA-62 (B-25) and Douglas B-23 – the Martin 179, soon designated B-26, scored a resounding victory. An engineering team led by young Peyton Magruder had turned out a beautiful machine that was a remarkable contrast to such Curtiss aircraft as the SBC-4, O-52 and even the new P-40 fighter. Martin conceded that it was unable to produce the required 385 bombers within the specified two-year period; therefore, the NAA contender won second prize of 184 airplanes. That was just as well. Ultimately the war lessons of Europe determined that a fully powered top turret should be installed, along with armor plate and self-sealing fuel tanks. Making its first takeoff on 25 November 1940, the Martin B-26 was powered by two new and powerful P&W R-2800 Double Wasp engines, the same type of engine specified for Republic's forthcoming XP-47B fighter. The medium bomber was able to attain a level-flight speed of 315 mph. Perhaps as remarkable was the fact that there was no real X-model version, the "prototype" being essentially a production airplane from an assembly line. Such a radical change from Depression times procedures was certain to create problems, particularly in a bomber with far higher wing loading than any known contemporary bomber (or fighter). The futuristic lines of the B-26 showed that a weapon could be beautiful as well as potent. In the meantime as the 179 early production phase progressed, Martin received a huge contract in May 1940 to produce the Martin Baltimore attack bomber, a successor to the Martin Maryland already being delivered to France.   *Martin*

BELOW In this remarkably rare color photograph of the Douglas XB-19 in flight, the bomber appears to be sitting on the horizon. During WWII, the bomber, like its cousin the XB-15, was cloaked in camouflage paint and was used to fly high-density cargoes between major air bases. Eventually if was flown to Cleveland, Ohio, where the Fisher Bomber Plant was located. There, it was modified with quick-engine-change Allison V-3420-11 engines. Early in 1946, it flew into Morrison Field, Florida, in the markings of the All Weather Flight Test Center, located at Clinton County Airport, Ohio. It is almost a certainty that B/Gen. Benjamin Kelsey, commanding officer of that organization was at the controls of the XB-19A airplane when it was parked at Morrison Field. *USAAC via Walter Boyne*

ABOVE Viewed at any significant distance, it was virtually impossible to distinguish between Boeing B-17C and D models. Outwardly, the only real visible difference, as of 1941 was in the engine cowlings; the C models did not have cooling flaps encircling the cowlings at the trailing edges. Not visible, of course, were the installations of self-sealing fuel tanks, armor plate at the crew stations, and later-model Wright R-1820-65 engines rated at 1000 horsepower. Boeing flew the first production B-17C on 21 July 1940 at Boeing Field. By the end of November, all of the thirty-eight C versions had been delivered from the still relatively small plant. Incredibly, on the very eve of 1941, the Army Air Corps was engaged in a serious dispute with Boeing about pricing of the airplanes. As a result, the company lacked funding for plant expansion that would improve efficiency and result in unit price reductions. The U.S. government had not yet figured out how the enormous plant expansions could be accomplished because no manufacturer was able or willing to assume huge debt with no guarantee that large orders would continue to follow for plant amortization. In an unprecedented move, especially at the hands of a "neutral" nation, the government released twenty of the B-17Cs to the British RAF. Boeing was authorized to apply British camouflage and insignia, serial numbers and equipment. Thus, the airplanes became Model 299Us prior to delivery. Since the remaining eighteen B-17Cs were evidently sans camouflage paint of any kind at time of delivery, all either remained unpainted or were painted by the Air Corps. One of the painted aircraft is seen here. *Nat. Archives*

(see photo)

(see photo)

BELOW During the period when Seversky P-35s and Curtiss P-36As were being delivered to the Army Air Corps in the last half of the '30s decade, the AAC invited manufacturers to enter a 1939 pursuit plane competition for what was billed a "High-altitude Fighter." The military authorized and funded conversion of the final plane on the P-35 contract for entry in the competition as the XP-41. This was a long-overdue improvement on the P-35 design, and one that should have been done – according to none other than B/Gen. Ben Kelsey – for service test analysis. It was a viable possibility in 1938, at least in part, for the Seversky sales tour of Europe that eventually resulted in a large order for two different models. Major de Seversky missed what appears to have been a golden opportunity by not first selling the idea to financier Moore, and then taking improved EP1 and 2PA models to England, the Continental countries and to Sweden. The good lines of the Seversky (not Republic) XP-41 at Langley Field show (see photo) what the P-35 could have been for a relatively small investment in 1936 or 1937. *NACA*

ABOVE Grumman finally got rolling on production of their F4F-3 Wildcats in 1940, but those carrier-based fighters still were not equipped with folding wings, and delays in deliver of the high-altitude P&W R-1830-76 (later, -86) engines were expected. Therefore, 100 of the 285 airplanes ordered as F4F-3s were equipped with one-speed, two-stage lower altitude engines. Again, the first 30 were built as British Martlet IIIs. Then 65 of the F4F-3A "transition trainers" were delivered to Marine Squadron VMF-111 and Navy squadrons starting on 10 April 1941, while deliveries of proper F4F-3s to Marine and Navy outfits began in August 1940. Service tests of the first two F4F-3s resulted in "beef up" the landing gear, replacement of the two cowling-position machine guns with four wing-mounted .50-caliber weapons and deletion of the large spinner used on the second production F4F-3. Propeller shank cuffs evidently solved the cooling deficiency. However, this F4F-3A, still chocked and with attending plane handler wearing a Pith helmet, was probably awaiting some signal to take off for participation in the 1941 Southern Louisiana Army-Navy maneuvers. Not widely known is the speed deficiency of F4F-3As relative to the F4F-3. Best altitude speed of the former at 16,000 feet was 312 mph while the –3s were rated at 331 mph at 21,300 feet. When Mitsubishi A6M2 Zero-Sen carrier-based fighters escorted the bombers on December 7, 1941, more than 400 of them were in service with the IJN. Why was the A6M2, with a top speed of only 317 mph at 16,400 feet, such a terror against USN fighters early on? Normal gross weight was only about 6,000 lbs. while the 1941 Wildcats grossed almost 8,000 pounds. *USMC*

Although the Grumman F4F-3A was altitude-limited because they were equipped with single-stage, two-speed supercharged engines, limiting their best rated power to about 16,000 feet, they saw early battle in the defense of Wake Island. Fortunately USMC Fighter Squadron VMF-211, based at Wake Island in the far Western Pacific, had a small number of Wildcats with which to confront Japanese bomber and fighter attacks. Of course the small defensive garrison was overwhelmed ultimately by far superior numbers. Handicapped from the start as they were by America's "No Foreign Entanglements" philosophy and its attendant budgetary effects in the 1930s, the Grumman Wildcats, like this VMF-121 Marine Corps F4F-3A, ultimately provided amazing service results during the entire course of the war. They deserve the same respect that British Fairey Swordfish torpedo biplanes have enjoyed for decades as fighting "ancient pelicans." When Grumman was constructing F4F Wildcats in a mix with J2F, JRF and J4F utility types, the factory appeared to be a helter-skelter assemblage of panic-stricken disorganization. American industry, especially the automobile manufacturing segment, came to the rescue in the form of its brand new Eastern Aircraft Division of General Motors. With civilian automobile production stopped, five East Coast factories began conversion to Wildcat production on 21 January 1942, test flying the first FM-1 Wildcat in August. GM eventually delivered 1151 of the -1 model before switching to the FM-2 model. Eastern Aircraft Division also produced hundreds of Grumman-designed TBF Avengers as TBMs.   *Rudy Arnold*

If some of the so-called first-line military aircraft involved in the 1941 Carolina War Games were still biplanes like this Curtiss SBC-4 from Bombing Squadron 8 escorted by three of our latest Grumman F4F-3 fighters, how could the military and naval forces feel confident? Here was a nation that had seen private individuals and tiny, struggling companies develop racing airplanes in the early 1930s that must have been the envy of Asiatic and European countries alike. Air racing in America in the Depression years was arguably progressive. Far more money was thrown into a single presidential election year than was spent on all racing aircraft development for the decade. But, by Armistice Day 1938, the United States of America was at best a fifth rate air power. Grumman, Curtiss and Bell were still building biplane naval fighters and bombers. Air Corps "heavy" bombers – except for a simple handful – were still slower than the commercial airliners of TWA, American Airlines and United Airlines. If a top general, such as in the cases of Billy Mitchell and Frank Andrews a decade apart, spoke out about the sorry state of our defenses he was drummed out or set aside to fret. The aircraft engine industry was on the verge of bankruptcy, possibly saved from extinction by France...of all countries. Now hear this! Every American battleship – there were sixteen – in the Navy until 1941 had been ordered between 1909 and 1917! Not one President of the USA between 1917 and 1937 had ever fought to order even one battleship until FDR authorized one in August 1937. Between 1937 and 1940 that single President – in the face of fierce Isolationist opposition – managed to order construction of **Seventeen.** The man must have been psychic. The fact that we are still free and alive, no matter what your political persuasion might be, certainly hinged on FDR's naval program to a major extent. And to his "off the cuff" 50,000 airplane program of that era.   *Hans Groenhoff*

Artfully photographed by a talented USMC photographer in the summer of 1941, this Vought SB2U-3 assigned to squadron VMSB-131 complied with all of the current 1941 BuAer painting directives to a tee. Although these Vindicators were handsome airplanes, they proved to be underpowered by the time they were called on to fight. They also had flight characteristics that prohibited their assignment to escort aircraft carriers such as USS *Charger* (AVG30). Britain's Royal Navy Fleet Air Arm quickly discovered this upon receiving Vought-Sikorsky V-156-B Chesapeake versions, a number of which had originally been ordered by France, and trying to adapt them to service aboard AVGs received via Lend-Lease. The SB2Us and V-156-Bs were designed to operate from USN fleet carriers having lengthy decks at least as large as the newest 1930s CV, the USS *Wasp.*   *USMC/NA*

RIGHT & BELOW   America, recovering from a devastating depression as 1940 dawned, was still probably the richest country in the world. Yet, on April 26, 1939, with war threatening in Europe and war already in progress in the Orient, what was the choice of our government as the main fighter aircraft for the oncoming global war? Nothing more than Donovan Berlin's 1934 design that had been thoroughly beaten in the April 1936 Wright Field competition, but ultimately wedded to the Air Corps' favored new Allison V-1710 engine. The 1939 competition winning XP-40 was nothing more than a standard Curtiss Aeroplane Division P-36A from the firewall aft to the rudder and wingtip to wingtip with an 1,150-hp inline, liquid-cooled engine installed. The competition from Seversky – the AP-4 and XP-41 – featured butt-skin plates with flush riveting, something never seen on the Curtiss P-40s. Total cost of the modification from P-36A to XP-40 was a mere $36,266.00, exclusive of GFE (engine and ancillary components). The so-called high-altitude competition was actually judged on performance at a measly 15,000 feet. Curtiss-Wright was awarded a contract for 524 of the P-40 airplanes, which pales to insignificance when one realizes that the corporation eventually built a total of 13,738 of these Type 81/87/P-40 production airplanes until the last P-40N model was delivered in November 1944! How many Curtiss Aeroplane Division Tomahawks, Kittyhawks, Warhawks/P-40s ever fought the *Luftwaffe* in the skies over Continental Europe? *NONE*! That, from the richest nation on earth. "Power corrupts; Absolute power corrupts absolutely." Does anyone really believe that a better management team could not have been forced on Curtiss-Wright during the course of our struggle for victory? Couldn't this nation have used far more Lockheed P-38s or North American P-51s? During the entire war, the complex but effective P-38 Lightnings were only built in quantity in one factory works. If the Buffalo factory,

properly managed, could have turned out 6000 Lightnings instead of nearly 14,000 Curtiss P-40/81/87 models, the cost factor would have been little more (not really an all-out war factor) until the last shots were in August 1945. Perhaps the Lightnings built there could have been Packard Merlin or Rolls-Royce Griffon powered for even better performance over *Festung Europa*. And finally, did the Truman Commission of Congress really do all that it could, and certainly at an earlier date, to stop whatever was really going on in Buffalo? Brewster Aeronautical was shut down hard in the midst of the war for no greater crimes than Curtiss-Wright committed. Republic Aviation's performance, in two factories, shows what can be done rapidly with proper managerial control. Mr. Ralph Damon proved that at Farmingdale. (The XP-40 flown at the Materiel Division remained in pre-war garb). Test pilots Herb Fisher and Ed Elliot are seen preparing to fly many Curtiss P-40s at Buffalo.   *Groenhoff via Richard Starinchak; Kerr via W. Thompson*

Joint maneuvers, some preferred to call them war games, conducted in the Deep South in 1941 were generally intended to sniff out weaknesses in military operations or, hopefully, show that strategies were on target. But the ground forces' hammerlock on military aviation had been far too firm for decades. Rather unexpectedly, one glaring example came from the use of the cheapest aircraft competing against some of the more expensive models. After two decades of procuring heavy 2- or 3-seat observation airplanes, frequently more powerful than the latest attack aircraft, a decision was made to test some steep-landing-and-takeoff airplanes specially constructed for front-line observation of troop movements and tactics. Stinson submitted the O-49, Bellanca entered the YO-50 and Ryan demonstrated the YO-51, all in 1940. Stinson received an initial order for 142 aircraft, with deliveries starting in the same year. Redesignated L-1, the airplanes participated in the maneuvers of 1941. Other manufacturers (Aeronca, Piper and Taylorcraft) also participated in the influx of orders for these liaison aircraft, while an order for Curtiss O-52's signaled the end of observation types as we had come to know them. This camouflaged North American O-47A was typical of 239 examples of the type procured for the AAC and National Guard between Fiscal Years 1936 and 1938, but the war games had the effect of turning them into little other than training planes. Those so-called "Grasshoppers" had rendered them obsolete. At the same time, they illustrated the hide-bound attitudes of infantry and artillery officers being those who dictated what was best for the AAC. By June 1941, that situation was on its way to the dump. *U.S. Army Air Force*

RIGHT and BELOW When a plethora of misleading, inventive reports followed the crash of the Lockheed XP-38 prototype in February 1939, it became nearly impossible to find the truth. Published reports suggested that the crash would set the P-38 programs back several years. B/Gen. Ben Kelsey certainly knew more about "behind the scenes" history of the P-38 than any other person, especially when he was a lieutenant reporting to M/Gen. Henry Arnold. Between them they managed to use the loss of that prototype to their

advantage. After all, Arnold was Chief of the Air Corps. They quickly convinced the Chief of Staff and congressional members to fund a service test order of thirteen Lockheed YP-38s. These airplanes, of which at least several were constructed in what had been the old G.G.G. Distillery located just north of Union Air Terminal in Burbank, were redesigned for what was then modest production (fewer than 100 airplanes). The switch to newer Allison F-series engines (V-1710F-2) was authorized in the July 1939 contract because Kelly Johnson's team had completed comprehensive improvement studies before the transcontinental flight. Some 19 months elapsed before the first YP flew. One or more YP-38s were tested with the 37-mm Browning M9 cannon, but nobody seemed very happy with that weapon or the gun mix. Ultimately, the weapons of choice would be the 20-mm Hispano-Suiza AN-M2 cannon and four .50-cal. Browning machine guns. In the meantime, French and British procurement authorities ordered at least 667 Model 322-B and 322-F fighters for just under $100 million. Since the new AAF had only ordered 65 of the P-38 and P-38D

types, and the British Direct Purchasing Commission took over the French order, major production emphasis was on the 322-B types for the Royal Air Force. The final 36 Model 222-62-08 series of the P-38 (no suffix letter) scheduled were to be completed as P-38Ds. An earlier order had designated all D-model Pursuit aircraft as being up to "combat" standards. Other than one experimental XP-38A, there were to be no P-38A through C models. This camouflaged P-38D was representing "Red forces" while participating in the 1941 summer maneuvers in the Carolinas. Only 36 of the new P-38Ds were delivered. At the time, eighty Bell P-39Cs were ordered, but 60 of those were built as P-39D models. The 31st Pursuit Group, 39th Pursuit Squadron Airacobras shown were almost certainly C models, never brought up to the D standard. Missing wheel cover plates were indicative of serious brake problems. *Nat. Archives via Gerry Markgraf (2)*

While the USS *Yorktown* (CV-5) was operating in Eastern waters in 1941, the carrier was newly equipped with Grumman F4F-3A Wildcat fighters. Three in formation were from Navy VF-5 serving in the Atlantic Ocean sector. The changeover from Grumman F3F biplane fighters to newer monoplanes came none too soon. Although the Brewster Aeronautical firm had beaten Grumman in obtaining orders for the latest in monoplane fighter aircraft, Grumman became the ultimate winner of USN contracts. In actual fact, within two years after the combined services war maneuvers were conducted, the government clamped a lid on Brewster for poor quality control and failure to meet production commitments. Here was another manufacturer with such poor product output that, in the dark days of the war, was effectively put out of business. Brewster's failure was a cancer on the Arsenal of Democracy. On the other hand, Grumman overcame their very poor start with the Wildcat development and produced an airplane that proved useful as a fighter against powerful Japanese forces until V-J Day in 1945. The type had also proven effective against Axis forces during the invasions of Sicily and Italy in the MTO. Just as remarkable was the role played by the Eastern Aircraft Division of General Motors in rapidly taking over the production load of Wildcats (as FM-1s and -2s) and Grumman Avengers. Changing quickly from automobile production to aircraft seemed to be taken in stride by GM. Amazing the aviation industry, the Division – involving five automobile factories – started from 'scratch' in April 1942 and initially manufactured FM-1 models for the USN and Royal Navy. Switching to an improved FM-2 version for better operational capability from the CVE and CVL escort and light carriers proliferating during the war, Eastern Aircraft turned out 4,127 of the FM-2s for the Navy and another 340 as Wildcat VIs for Great Britain. It was a magnificent performance attributable to good management and industrious workers. *USN/NA*

Long before the war in Europe erupted in September 1939, factions within the U.S. Army Air Corps had been engaged in what seemed to amount to a small war was being fought among the various components of that service over camouflage on aircraft. Tests seemed to go on forever. Way back in 1933, a Technical Order (T.O.) pertaining to tactical camouflage had been issued. Many tests were conducted over the years, and battles seemed to stem from all. General Arnold finally approved a suggestion in 1940, and a camouflage specification was issued. All of this was detailed in a revised T.O. 07-1-1 in April 1941. However, in February, it had been concluded that there was an urgent need to camouflage all new and existing B-17 bombers. Since Boeing was losing about $10,000 on every plane delivered, the company made a bid that was characterized by the AAC as "exorbitant quotations" for the camouflaging. The work was assigned to Sacramento Air Depot until July 1, 1941; after that, Boeing was to do the painting. By that time, the new U.S. Army Air Force was created in June 1941. This perfect side elevation of B-17E "Chief Seattle" shows the optimum markings prevailing prior to the attack on the United States by Japan on December 7. *USAAF*

BELOW Buffalo, NY, can be bitterly cold in mid winter. Those icy-cold days when there is crunchy snow under foot and a nearly cloudless blue sky overhead can be especially memorable if you are on an airport. While a Curtiss-built P-40 might have inspired confidence in the public eye in the winter months of 1940, the fall of France and the Battle of Britain seen on Fox Movietone newsreels in every theater in the country should have given any observer pause. The XP-40 had been touted in magazines and newspapers as a "400-mph fighter" in 1939, but our confidence had to really be placed in the ocean expanses between America and Asia or Europe. Only illusionary thoughts could now convince us that the Nazis were not far better prepared for warfare than we. Our British friends of long standing were teetering on the brink of disaster, like it or not. If the British Isles could not be successfully invaded, they surely could be starved into surrender. One sensed that the main asset held by the British was America's Arsenal of Democracy. Their French allies were gone, and all of *Festung Europa* was overrun with the German military machine. To the south, the Italians were at least a thorn in the side. A goodly number of U.S. Navy Curtiss SBC-4 dive bombers (like the two seen in the background) were being "transferred" to the French government, eventually winding up on the carrier *Bearn* reposing in Martinique waters in the West Indies. They were doomed to sit out the war, rotting away in a climate far warmer than Buffalo enjoyed. If any Curtiss SBC-4 ever fired a shot or dropped a bomb in anger, it was a well-kept secret. The French surrender in June 1940 came far too soon for the hordes of Curtiss Model 81 and Lockheed 322-F fighters to have done the *Armee de l'Air* a bit of good. Those procurement actions came much too late to become anything but saber rattling. *Jack Kerr via W. Thompson*

ABOVE In contrast to a typical "Hurry up and wait" attitude in 1940, the Bureau of Aeronautics of the USN seemed to have a chosen a path to "Wait and then hurry up" with regard to a replacement for the slow Douglas TBD-1 torpedo plane. In retrospect, it appears that the USN should have begun a program in about 1939 to upgrade the existing airplanes with more powerful versions of the R-1830 Twin Wasps in place of the 900 hp units installed in production. Even without the semi-externally mounted torpedo the best speed shown by a TBD-1 was no better than that of a North American SNJ-5 with 550 hp. The prototype Grumman XTBF-1 (see photo) began life with nearly double the power available in the TBD-1, but gross weight was only up about 50 percent. Both planes were to carry and launch the same standard naval torpedo. Unfortunately for Americans, the IJN Nakajima B5N2 torpedo bombers were faster and carried a far more effective and reliable torpedo, perhaps the weapon being the determining factor in mission performance. On August 1, 1941, the XTBF-1 took to the air for the first time, just about fifteen months after the BuAer issued a contract for two prototypes. Grumman had no experience at all in development of torpedo or bombing aircraft, but urgency seemed to be the thing needed to avoid the prolonged development time associated with the F4F Wildcat. Fortunately for all concerned, a production contract for 286 airplanes had been issued seven months before the prototype flew. One evident change between the XTBF-1 and the production airplanes was addition of a dorsal fin that remained unchanged over the entire life of Avenger airplanes. USN acceptance of the prototype occurred within days of the Pearl Harbor attack, and the first production airplane came off the line just about one month later. A backup design, the Vought XTBU-1 Sea Wolf looked very good, but even when development and production was transferred to Consolidated Aircraft the type never became operational. *Grumman*

In the middle of the 1930s decade, when Boeing, Douglas, Northrop, Curtiss, Consolidated, etc. were deeply involved in production of all-metal aircraft, Vought Division of the United Aircraft Corporation found itself far behind the state-of-the-art. Northrop Aircraft, on the other hand, had pioneered in stressed-skin, monocoque aluminum construction. At least one executive at Vought's plant in East Hartford, Conn., recognized that the tubular metal structure with attached aluminum panels and some fabric-covered portions of an airplane were obsolete. However, Vought was manufacturing nearly 250 new SB2U series scout bombers for the USN and the V-156's for the French *Aeronaval*. In fact, the fuselage structure of the SB2U-1 through -3 and V-156-F1 was essentially an elongated version of the one used on Navy SBU-1 biplanes of 1935 vintage. The SB2U-1 was one of the USN's first carrier-based monoplanes adopted as a standard type. Three separate orders for production versions of the XSB2U-1 totaled 169 airplanes delivered for first-line duty with the Atlantic Fleet and the U.S. Marine Corps. Most of the SB2U-3 Vindicators, like this one assigned to VMSB-131, went to two USMC squadrons. Some took part in the Battle of Midway. Almost immediately thereafter, they were withdrawn from combat service. Possibly as a result of an appearance of a tastefully presented V-156 demonstrator at the 1938 *Salon de l' Aeronautique*, the French Purchasing Commission ordered 20 examples of the Vought bomber. These airplanes, designated as V-156-F3s, were actually delivered to France, but several fell into German hands as the French Republic went down under the *Wehrmacht* and *Luftwaffe* onslaught. By direct purchase, the British acquired an undelivered French commitment for 50 aircraft under the designation V-156-BI for the Royal Naval Air Service. It was soon recognized that flight operations from so-called "Jeep" escort carriers was not practical because the Chesapeakes required lengthy takeoff runs. Can United Aircraft be blamed for selling an airplane designed to operate from Saratoga-sized carriers if the purchasers did not specify certain flight requirements? The answer is obvious.   *USMC*

BELOW, RIGHT and OPPOSITE   Designed at the Curtiss Buffalo plant, the XP-46/-46A fighters could quite easily have been the inspiration for some of the fighters quickly designed and built in Russia in the days when the USSR was being invaded by the Nazi forces. At least the concepts were very close. The toothless XP-46A proved to be a little faster than contemporary P-40s, all of which were armed and armored. Curtiss-Wright was not about to give up, but was certainly suffering from a bad dose of lethargy. With no chance of producing P-46s, they wangled a contract for a new design Model 90 (military XP-60), starting as a modified P-40D. Therefore, they jumped backwards to the Model 75 of half a decade earlier. The Curtiss division was proving it was not likely to be a pacesetter. Contracts were awarded to the division to produce duplicates of Republic Thunderbolts, which they did so badly that P-47G-CUs never went beyond training schools. But the Republic design further polluted engineering's thinking, assuring the eventual P-60s would be later-day spin-offs of the Republic fighter. The end of Curtiss as an airplane division was appearing on the distant horizon.   *J.Kerr via W. Thompson (3)*

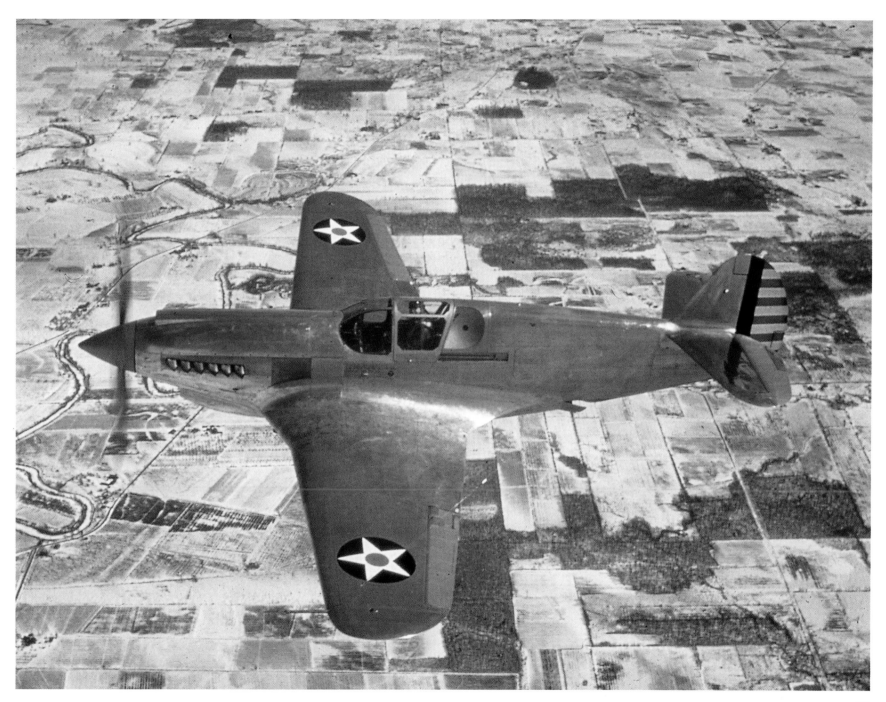

France's experience with the Curtiss H75-A fighter, even though the type was obsolescent at the time an order for 100 was placed in 1938, turned out to be a quality move. Compared to the main first-line fighters available from French constructors, namely the Dewoitine D.520 and the Morane-Saulnier M.S.406, the 1,200 horsepower versions of the Curtiss H75-A were stronger, longer ranging and every bit as fast as the D.520. The M.S.406 was essentially a short-range interceptor with fuselage construction on a par with Curtiss P-6E biplane fighters. When the *Armee de l'Air* finally had the opportunity to purchase the equivalent of the USAAC Curtiss P-40 via direct purchase, they eagerly ordered 100 copies as H81-As. Akin to the orders for Lockheed 322-Fs, the orders were too late and too little. The first H81-A export model was ready for delivery in March 1940; it never even got to France, which capitulated to the Nazis in the first days of June. Subsequently, the British absorbed the French orders, calling the aircraft Tomahawks. Eventually, the British received well over 1,000 Tomahawks and used them well in North Africa. In the meantime, the Curtiss Aeroplane Division had been awarded a development contract for two Model 86 airplanes bearing the basic designation XP-46. (The second article was the XP-46A, built without armament and other equipment installed in the first airframe.) Republic Aviation had designed their AP-10 – or XP-47 – along similar lines. Both manufacturers use Allison F-series engines in their respective designs. Originally intended as lighter-weight fighters than earlier designs such as the P-40s, it was not to be the case. The European war showed the need for self-sealing fuel tanks, armor plate and armor glass, plus heavier armament. Results: An XP-46 was not even one percent faster than the P-40. It just had a prettier face. *Jack Kerr via W. Thompson*

90

It may come as a surprise to many, but numerous North American AT-6 airplanes in the earliest series actually began life categorized as BC-1As. They won out over the pretty Vultee BC-3. Now, encounter this situation: NAA's Y1BT-10 was essentially a BT-9 fitted with a 600 hp R-1340 engine, produced in small quantity for the USN as the NJ-1. Along came the AAC's North American BC-1, being for all the world like the NJ-1 except for some rudder mods and having a retractable landing gear. Essentially, the Air Corps obtained 180 of the BC-1s before war erupted in Europe. North American went to an all-metal fuselage for the BC-2 with its 3-blade propeller, only to create a BC-1A from best features of the BC-1 and BC-2…if you follow me. They ordered 92 of the BC-1As, but soon abandoned the Basic Combat category, and settled on the AT-6 as an Advanced Trainer. Yes, it can be confusing, especially when the Navy's SNJ models are interjected into the melee. Of course we could point out that the British Harvards, as Mk. I and II, can dirty the waters even more. Suffice to say, the AT-6 Texan series amounted to thousands of aircraft for everyone but the Nazis and the Japanese. But wait, weren't those Japanese fighters and dive bombers in the movies AT-6 look-alikes? Of course. (Those AT-6/SNJs will outlast me – Auth.) The AT-6A seen here is AC41-306, to be accurate. *AAF/R. Starinchak*

In prewar days and evidently well into wartime, certain training aircraft assigned to USN major training bases wore bright and interesting color schemes. Such is the case with this rather typical North American NJ-1, a "spin-off" from the Army Air Corps' BT-9C. Since the Navy at that time did not want a Wright engine, the AAC – in a spirit of cooperation – had one BT-9C developed under the Y1BT-10 service test designation. North American powered it with a Pratt & Whitney R-1340 engine producing 200 hp more than was available in any BT-9 model. That power increase raised the top speed to 198 mph, close to that demonstrated by the Air Corps' NAA BC-1 equipped with a retractable landing gear. BuAer then made its first North American Aviation trainer buy, a purchase of forty NJ-1s. A USN machinist's mate is seen preparing an NJ-1 for flight at NAS Pensacola.   *USN via R. Starinchak*

Dominant Curtiss-Wright Corp. hoped to supplant all the their SBC-3 and –4 biplane dive bombers manufactured at Buffalo, N.Y., by producing their modern-looking monoplane, the XSB2C-1, powered – of course – by a 1600-hp Wright R-2600 Cyclone engine. It was only when I was writing this book that I began to understand why the U.S. Navy was so determined to make the SB2C Helldiver a useful weapon. The actual original design emanated from BuAer in conjunction with the Naval Aircraft Factory in 1937. Curtiss built the first XSB2C-1 in 1939. It was damaged beyond repair in landing when it broke in half in the winter of 1940-41. The USN did not get its second prototype XSB2C-1 (seen here) until 1942. Curtiss proved itself to be almost totally inept at creating a new aircraft of any type subsequent to the start of WWII in September 1939 despite turning out a virtual stream of prototypes.   *Curtiss via R. Starinchak*

Although it must be conceded that work clothes have not necessarily changed much in sixty years, few engineers or executives are likely to dress in the fashion seen on such a person as one in this flightline snapshot circa 1941. Fedora hats for men are essentially a thing of the past. Such soft felt hats virtually disappeared in the 1950s decade. Current costs alone would make them unpopular, with even a cheap version most like selling for over $100. But more to the point is the astounding change in GSE (ground support equipment). The tractor in this picture was merely a slight derivative of any gasoline-powered farm tractor of that era. These Curtiss-Wright employees do not seem to be unduly bothered by snow-covered tarmac or concrete aprons and the bitterly cold winds that can blow in from the Great Lakes. If that is not enough to support the time element, the SBC-4's are.   *Jack Kerr via W. Thompson*

Douglas Aircraft, with the assistance of Boeing Aircraft in Seattle, Washington, produced much-improved versions of the original Douglas 7B prototypes, one of which created a cause célèbre when the attack plane crashed at Mines Field, Calif., killing the pilot and a French Air Attaché aboard the "Secret" aircraft. It was in the era of political isolationism; the aircraft had not even been divulged to the public, but there was a foreign military man aboard the 7B light bomber. That was a total reversal of existing policy. The original design was from John Northrop's former shops south of Imperial Highway, across from North American Aviation's new factory in Inglewood. Northrop Corporation was actually a subsidiary of Douglas until 1937 when Donald Douglas (51% stockholder) wished to make that plant the El Segundo Division of Douglas. He did. Northrop struck out on his own once again, wanting to express his own design philosophies. Undeterred by the crash of the 7B, France ordered 105 examples of an improved version (the DB-7) redesigned and manufactured at Santa Monica. Douglas dedicated the El Segundo Division to building naval aircraft. By October 1939, the French Purchasing Commission placed a second, larger order for 165 more powerful versions of the light bomber. A fine warplane was born, but it was too late for France. Bostons and the offspring Havocs did serve the RAF and the AAF well, however. The Arsenal of Democracy was doing its bit.   *NA via Richard Starinchak*

94

What is wrong with this picture? Seemingly, nothing. But why would the first article airplane of the second British contract for Mustang Is, camouflaged in typical RAF camouflage paint, carry U.S. national markings with British serial number AL958? Unless, of course, it is a fraud. But only in the context of publicity like the NA-73X with Air Corps tail stripes – which lasted all of four hours. NAA's Contract Report "O" plus official RAF records confirm that all AL, AM and AP serial numbered Mustangs were shipped to the Royal Air Force on Contract A-1493, issued just four months after the first contract. The only valid answer is that AL958 was given "Star and Meatball" markings just five weeks after its first flight on 23 April 1941. Remember that the new Army Air Force came into being on 1 June 1941! The so-called 'Smoking Gun' syndrome. Not a few people have been fooled. It existed long enough for a selection of Kodchrome 1 photographs to be created. The first contract for P-51s was one of those Defense Aid for Britain contracts, DA-140, issued ten months after the second British contract. Without that marvelous "O" report, it would be almost impossible to follow the trail. The NA-83 airplanes were "refined" Mustang I fighters for England. A second real clue was in the Sand and Spinach camouflage paint scheme. We can only hope all 320 Mustang I airplanes reached English ports. *L of C Office of War Information*

The North American Mustang story has been told many times in many ways. It is sometimes difficult to separate the facts from voluminous fiction. The primary thing to consider is that its development was a marvelous achievement at the right time, and we owe much to the wartime people at Rolls-Royce's Hucknall facility in England. The part played by those engineers and technicians and by AAF Major Thomas Hitchcock in converting a successful fighter airplane (RAF's first production Mustang shown) into a major star is almost beyond comprehension. However great the P-51Ds and Ks were in that conflict, they were not uppermost. Other great American fighter stars in WWII were Lockheed's P-38 Lightning, Republic's P-47 Thunderbolt, Vought's F4U Corsair, and Grumman's F6F Hellcat. We know that Grumman F4F/FM Wildcats, Bell P-39 Airacobras and the Curtiss P-40s were indispensable at certain times and locations, but they could never have gained air superiority in many key theaters throughout the war. Two fighter aircraft situations have always puzzled this author, and explanations of the whys and wherefores have been totally lacking. First, why was the complex P-38 not given a second production source early in the conflict, and why did the War Production Board fail to allow production of P-38s with Merlin engines at such a source? Second, with Packard getting approval for plant expansion to manufacture R-R Merlin engines in America for Great Britain in August 1940, why didn't the British Purchasing Commission insist on using a Merlin engine in the Mustang right from the start? When it did happen ultimately, it made a pretty good airplane great. The first Mustangs could have received some U.K. production allocations of Merlins from the start. An opportunity was there. The RAF had no experience with Allison engines at high altitudes, especially over *Festung Europa*. As for the Lightning, Kelly Johnson's engineers had completed significant studies and preliminary design engineering for just such a program. That was more than ample reason to second-source the Lightning. Bill Kundsen's OPM-WPB didn't allow it. *NAA via Robt. Archer*

BELOW   This gathering of early Curtiss P-40s as first-line fighters of the U.S. Army's GHQ Air Force reveals the tragic effect an isolational-biased American Congress and self-serving military leaders can have on our military and naval strength. Publicity in less-than-honest aviation magazines and various news media gave Americans a distorted picture of our defensive and offensive stature as compared to prospective enemies in 1941. The Curtiss P-40 is a prime example. The wartime (1944) Truman Committee reports spoke out very well – but did anybody really listen? They criticized the Curtiss P-40 program on a number of points. For example: Massive original procurement of an inadequate, obsolete airframe that was far from state-of-the-art. Yet, the type remained continuously in production for – at minimum – a dozen months after production should have been terminated. Also, the Truman report stated that far better fighters were in production. (Again it must be emphasized that the proposed R-R Merlin-powered P-38 could have gone into production in 1942. However, the WPB never authorized a second production facility until the war was nearly won.) In the meantime, General Kenney in the far Southwest Pacific area was begging for P-38s but could only get small numbers because of ETO (9AF) and MTO (15AF) requirements. Consider this: If the Curtiss P-36 could be "hot-rodded" with an Allison V-1710 to create the XP-40, just visualize the P-38 with two Rolls-Royce Griffons of more than 2000 hp each installed. Even the little Supermarine Spitfires eventually served nicely with Griffons installed, displaying speeds equaling the best Merlin P-51s. A Griffon-powered Lightning could probably have attained speeds into compressibility in level flight with more than 4000 hp on tap. One can only speculate on the reasons for WPB ignoring such logic, but Curtiss-Wright continued P-40 manufacturing unabated until the line was finally shut down in mid-November 1944. With that in mind, think of the ridiculous action of finally taking the Vultee A-35B Vengeance out of production (long overdue) at Nashville about D-Day 1944. Then they began to tool the plant for P-38L-5-VE with production starting in January 1945. After producing only 113 examples by June, the WPB terminated production. A sad commentary on certain war efforts.   *Air Corps via G. Markgraf*

ABOVE   Although the new, advanced Martin B-26 Marauder was more difficult to construct than the competing North American B-25 Mitchell, the Maryland company did yeoman work in getting numerous examples of the basic early production bombers into flight status by the spring of 1941. It was no simple task. Lessons learned from the war in Europe, especially during the Battle of Britain, had to be reflected in the new bombers. Among things needed were a powered top turret, improvements in the tail-gun position, armor plate at strategic locations and the all-important self-sealing fuel tanks. Of course empty and gross weights increased, affecting flight performance. Some compensating changes could not be included in the early airplanes delivered to the 22BG at Langley Field, Virginia, the initial unit receiving the Marauders. Some, certainly not all, of those early B-26s were rushed to Australia soon after the Pearl Harbor attack. (As a matter of fact, one of those initial B-26s found its way to the "school yard" at Aero I.T.I. in Glendale, Calif., about a year later. Aero I.T.I. was, by then, one of the many mechanics' training schools operated by civilian contractors for the AAF. For company, the B-26 had everything from Douglas O-38s and Boeing P-26Cs to YP-38 gondola center sections.) As it is with most new products rushed prematurely into the most strenuous service, component failures were rampant. The Curtiss Propeller Division of C-W was late in deliveries, affecting both Martin B-26s and Lockheed P-38s. (As Marauders rolled from the Middle River Plant 2 that had been constructed hurriedly under the impetus of Arsenal of Democracy pressures, another huge Martin plant was constructed for B-26 production near Omaha, Nebraska.) One of the early Model 179 bombers awaits its turn to fly, while two pilots discuss plans for that and other testing. Concurrently with B-26 production, Martin built hundreds of their Model 187 (Baltimore and A-30) upgrade of the earlier Maryland for France and Great Britain at Middle River, Maryland. *Martin via Widewing*

It is interesting to discover that the Bell XP-39 was delivered by rail to Wright Field on or about December 27, 1938, while the Lockheed XP-38 was delivered by roadway, arriving at March Field, Calif., within the week on New Year's Day, 1939. a unique coincidence. The XP-39 made its initial flight at Wright Field on April 6, 1939 – after numerous delays – several months after the XP-38's initial flight on 27 January 1939. Bell test pilot James Taylor was first to fly the XP-39, but Capt. Ben Kelsey flew it subsequently. When he landed, he calmly told Larry Bell and Robert Woods that "it was the most dynamically unstable pursuit plane he had ever flown." He suggested several corrective actions. Because the situation in Europe was changing rapidly, it is probable that Gen. Arnold had concluded that Ben had a big job guiding the P-38 program, so Capt. George Price was assigned as P-39 Project Officer. It appears that NACA engineers convinced Price that deleting the G.E. turbosupercharger would solve overabundant drag problems. In the face of multitudinous concurrent staffing problems and expansion, there were many cases of failed coordination. Of course Price did not make the decision unilaterally, but obviously Kelsey, out of the XP-39 loop in late 1939, raised serious objections to turbocharger removal. (In fact Kelsey was ordered to England as aide to Col. Carl 'Tooey' Spaatz with orders to evaluate equipment, training, combat tactics and performance. The duo arrived at Hendon Airport, London, on 31 May 1940 via Italy and France even as the Dutch, Belgian and French Armies and the *Armee de l'Air* failed.)   That single action doomed the P-39 type to a role absolutely contrary to Kelsey's original intentions. When Hitler's forces overwhelmed Western Europe in about one month, the entire world was thrown into confusion. In service at Selfridge Field, Mich., in 1941, these P-39Ds of the 31st Pursuit Group were faced with many deficiencies inherent in the Airacobra design. They included, of course, range and best operational altitude limitations. The "War Games" in the Deep South that summer did nothing to mitigate the situation. *AAF via Robt. D. Archer*

Stemming from results obtained through service evaluation of the Curtiss A-18As, 2-engine attack aircraft, an Air Corps competition was conducted in 1938 for a new twin-engine attack-bomber. North American Aviation's entry was the NA-40, soon modified to NA-40B. That entry crashed and did not win the competition, but it was the progenitor of the B-25 Mitchell medium bomber entry for the CP39-640 design competition. Both Martin and NAA came out of that event as winners with the B-26 and B-25 (NA-62) airplanes. Armament was overly light, but a transparent clamshell tail gun station on the B-25 boasted a .50-cal. Browning gun. The tail gun station only existed on the two-dozen B-25 airplanes and forty B-25As of the initial contract for 184 bombers (Martin received the key order for 201 of the B-26s). As revealed by this early B-25B in flight (sans any tail number or guns), a Martin top turret replaced the tail gun position. Smooth-surface engine cowls indicate use of a single outboard exhaust stack for each R-2600-9 engine. Externally the B-25 Mitchell transparent-nose versions retained a remarkable sameness in appearance through the war. The turret moved forward later on, waist gun positions were improved and a two-gun tail station was created. *Gene Boswell via G. Balzer*

It is probable that the NAA B-25B pictured (AC40-2344) is one of the Doolittle "Tokyo Raiders" of 1942. The airplane reveals updated cowlings with Clayton S-type flame-damping exhaust stacks, first fitted to B-25C-15-NA bombers. Another clue to the mission is the "20-mm cannon" installed in the Plexiglas tail cone. The "gun" was a dummy, actually a broom handle. Maj. James Hilger (later B/Gen.) who commanded the second group of eight "Tokyo Raider" bombers confirmed that subterfuge at a much later date. The totally unexpected, much needed "morale-booster" raid on Japan was a huge uplifting event in a period of almost constant defeats on the Western Pacific and SWPA battlefronts in 1942. Of all bombers, only the B-25s could have performed the feat, launching from a small 20,000-ton aircraft carrier, the U.S.S. *Hornet* (CV-8) on 18 April 1942. Sadly, the *Hornet* was lost in the Battle of Santa Cruz on October 26.   *NAA via G. H. Balzer*

The Better Half, referring, of course, to the new aft fuselage of the B-17E, a more effective replacement for the B-17D Flying Fortress. Great success was not to be realized at the time (1941) with the remotely aimed, unmanned belly turret design created by Bendix. This first B-17E (Model 299-O) was equipped with that new Bendix belly turret, aimed from a prone sighting station several feet aft of the turret that was mounted immediately behind the wing trailing edge. The two Browning machine guns could traverse laterally 360 degrees and be depressed almost vertically down from horizontal. The turret itself was no larger than the manned top turret. That remote type turret was installed on the first 112 new B-17Es built, but sighting proved to be difficult for most gunners. A manned ball turret replaced it on all subsequent B-17s. Overall length of the B-17E increased just one inch shy of six feet, and design maximum gross weight advanced from 47,560 pounds to 48,730 pounds. Of course the top speed of the B-17E was slightly reduced (by 6 mph) – from the 327 mph speed claimed for the B-17D model – because of the additional aerodynamic drag and weight attributable to the power turrets and enlarged tailplane. That length and increased fin/dorsal fin area provided additional resistance to "Dutch roll" during steady-state bombing runs. Incidentally, the aircraft pictured (AC41-2393) is the only B-17E to fly in the combat configuration without camouflage paint. *Boeing via P. M. Bowers*

In the days before the Japanese attacks on Pearl Harbor, TH, and the American installations in the Philippine Islands, there were considerable contentious dealings between Boeing and the Chief of the Air Corps, Materiel Command, and the Secretary of War over payment for production of B-17 bombers. Without contracts and payment, Boeing could hardly be expected to accept new orders for the Flying Fortresses and order long-delivery-time materials and equipment. It was also a period in which no program existed for financing construction of new or expanded factories to handle the tremendous influx of new orders. Frankly, most manufacturers lacked the financial wherewithal to commit themselves to rapid expansion. But here we have Boeing developing and producing a new combat-capable version of the B-17, having to expand tremendously while "bean counters" argued almost vociferously over prices and funding. It must be remembered that it was an election year, Continental Europe was almost entirely under Nazi occupation, but many Americans were isolationist in their viewpoints. That was hardly a positive atmosphere in which raging expansion of the military, navy and industry could operate effectively. The capitulation of all Europe and Japanese aggression against China, not to mention the Russian attack on Finland most certainly jarred large numbers of Americans into common sense reality. This camouflaged B-17E was becoming typical of the dull colors, which would prevail over Americans for at least six years. In this situation, **B**oeing alone constructed 512 of the new B-17Es. Within a short time the B-17 originator was joined by others in building Flying Fortresses. **V**ega (Lockheed) and **D**ouglas became B-17 builders (thus generating the B-V-D acronym, as in underwear).   *USAF via Robt. D. Archer*

Although the Army Air Corps had dabbled in the "science" of aircraft camouflage during most of the 1930s decade, it appeared to be more for publicity than for serious disguise. Most of the efforts were directed at use of water-soluble paints, somewhat easily removed after some undefined time. For aviation photographers, it was akin to having a wonderful smorgasbord of foods offered without restrictions. Application and short-term display continued into 1940. With the war in Europe destined, in the minds of many, to engulf America, some serious proclamations (specifications, etc.) were issued for camouflage, but the AAF and USN went in entirely different directions. The British were considerably better at camouflage, but even they were frequently inclined toward change. On December 8, 1941, it seems like scattershot became the way of life. With the new AAF far from ready for a shooting war, there was a dire need for airplanes. The U.S. government immediately commandeered many airplanes on order for the British or awaiting resolution of British contract cancellations, e.g., the Lockheed 322-B and Bell Model 14 Airacobra I. A large number of Lend-Lease aircraft were quickly impressed into AAF service for defense or training purposes. The huge influx of new recruits could have overwhelmed the systems otherwise. Equipment was needed, and needed immediately. That really threw the camouflage situations into chaos. Here we have an "impressed" Lockheed Model B 14 Hudson swathed in an RAF paint scheme, but marked with formal American national insignias. The A-29B-LO was supposed to be a photographic-duty-only airplane, one of 24 conversions. However, it had a British Boulton Paul power turret armament configuration. It seems that an A-29's open gun station setup would be better for air-to-air photography. The Hudson program was a roaring success for tiny Lockheed, catapulting it from a weak company to one of the top manufacturers. From December 1938 until July 1943, Lockheed produced no less than 2941 examples of Model 414 Hudsons under a variety of designations. Add to that 112 Model 14 Super Electras manufactured at Burbank.   *Lockheed*

When Fiscal Year 1940 came around, it was time to buy replacements for the well worn BT-9 series basic trainers. This time North American Aviation's healthy replacement for them was in the form of an all-metal BT-14. It had a significant top speed margin over the Vultee entry, but the BT-13 was probably cheaper. Another factor was involved. The War Department most likely looked at the major production commitment connected to BC-1A/AT-6/SNJ trainers being built for the AAC, USN and trainers for the British, not to mention the large B-25 commitment and British orders for the NA-73 fighters. It seemed more logical to give Vultee a large BT-13 trainer order, so the BT-14 production was only about equal to the number of various BT-9 models to be replaced. In any event, the airplane was close to being a lower-powered version of the AT-6 with a fixed landing gear. Apparently most BT-14s were assigned to Randolph Field, Texas. The airplane depicted is a 52nd School Squadron BT-14, nicely decked out in the prewar AAC colors, which remained in effect at Randolph for many months after December 7, 1941. *Fred Bamberger*

Two important entities involved in the overall Arsenal of Democracy appear in this picture of a USN North American SNJ-1 flying at funnel height as the destroyer USS *Drayton* (DD366) steams rapidly in the opposite direction. The destroyer was also known as the "Blue Beetle" in acknowledgement of its strange camouflage paint job. *Drayton* was serving in the Atlantic Fleet at the time. It is quite likely that the SNJ-1 Texan was operating with a photographic training unit at NAS Pensacola, Florida. A small Navy Yard existing south of the town of Pensacola was home for an aviation unit beginning on 20 January 1914. With seven aircraft on hand, the first flight from the yard took place on 2 February 1914 with Lt. John H. Towers (Naval Aviator No. 3) and Ensign G. deC. Chevalier (Naval Aviator No. 7) at the controls. Pensacola was designated as a Naval Air Station in December 1917. The NAS grew extremely rapidly during WWII. With several satellite air stations nearby, the training base graduated approximately 28,000 naval aviators, including 2,775 British pilots and some USAAF pilots. The base itself was a major training facility for flying boat pilots. *USN/NA*

Scout-Observation class airplanes for the USN are best exemplified by the Curtiss SOC-series airplanes, initially ordered as an XO3C-1 in June 1933. The SO prefix was adopted in 1934 when scouting and observation duties were combined. Previously, observation airplanes operated from battleships, while scouting aircraft were deployed on cruisers. Incredibly, although the Curtiss SOC Seagull type joined the Fleet in 1934, they were still operating in small numbers aboard ship more than a decade later when Japan surrendered in 1945. In the meantime, a new Vought XOS2U-1 monoplane prototype Observation-Scout (OS type) passed muster in 1938, with the BuAer ordering 54 examples. Production OS2U-1 Kingfisher aircraft began reaching the Fleet in August 1940. They served aboard ship with float gear, alternating with fixed wheel gear for shore duty assignments. Before production ceased in 1942, OS2U deliveries from Vought-Sikorsky Division of UAC totaled 1218 airplanes. The Naval Aircraft Factory manufactured 300 additional Kingfishers under the designation OS2N-1 (co-equal to OS2U-3 airplanes). These three V-S OS2U-1s were deployed with Navy Observation Squadron 3, based aboard the battleship USS *Mississippi.* The lead Kingfisher later served aboard the USS *New Mexico,* but was lost at sea on 4 November 1941. A competitor ordered by the USN, the Curtiss SO3C type (SO for Scout Observation), was powered by an inverted vee, Ranger V-770 engine. Vought-Sikorsky produced a direct competitor somewhat akin to the OS2U series, but this bird was designated XSO2U-1 as if to confuse the entire issue. Unfortunately, it too had Ranger power, and no production contract was awarded. On the other hand, the Navy Department had the audacity to purchase a total of 795 Curtiss SO3C-1 Seamews over a period of 18 months, only to suddenly withdraw all from service early in 1944. In the meantime, they provided no fewer than 250 to the Royal Navy as SO3C-2s. Typical of many Curtiss designs in WWII, the Seamew was a flying disaster. Many British and USN Seamews served as aerial targets – if and when they could get them airborne. The type was an investigative target of the wartime Truman Committee, as well it should have been. Curtiss-Wright Corporation deserved a full congressional investigation, with replacement of management a primary consideration. Mr. Ralph Damon would have been an ideal man to take the top management job, but it was not even suggested. Curtiss Airplane Division was allowed to obstruct justice throughout the war. Sadly, incompetence was rewarded. Obviously the "watchdogs" had no teeth. On the other hand, V-S OS2U Kingfishers provided good service up until the war ended. *via Jim Sullivan*

Even before America was thrust into the World War scene, USN and Coast Guard aircraft were armed to attack any enemy submarine spotted within the 3-mile limit or attacking any American vessel – even outside that limit. Therefore, the so-called scout-observation Vought-Sikorsky OS2U Kingfishers were being armed with depth charges, unofficially turning them into scout-bombers. It was only natural that pilots in training at Pensacola would have to receive training in the art of dropping depth charges for effect. This uncamouflaged Kingfisher (probably an OS2U-1) is seen with 325-lb. depth charge bombs carried on underwing shackles. *USN*

As early as February 3, 1937, the USN Training Command became interested in the Air Corps' new basic trainer, the BT-9, especially in the –9B configuration except for the Wright engine. In a then unusually cooperative action, the one and only Army Y1BT-10 – a BT-9C converted with a P&W Wasp R-1340 engine producing 550 hp vs. the normal BT-9's Wright 400 hp unit – was transferred to the USN. Tested at the Naval Aircraft Factory, it proved to be just what the Navy wanted. As a result, forty BT-9Bs built on Air Corps contract AC-9345 were modified with the Wasp engines and transferred to the money-strapped Navy as NJ-1s by Change Order #2198. Most, if not all, NJ-1s were employed as instrument trainers. Ultimately, the Air Corps procured a version equipped with retractable landing gear and a flat-bottom rudder, but the basic fabric-covered fuselage was retained. Navy liked the performance and ordered yet another cross-breed with all-metal fuselage, cropped wingtips and the 600 hp Wasp engine. So many versions, so much confusion! Rarely has anyone accurately defined all of the Texan (primarily AT-6/SNJ) trainers. Even the Japanese bought one NA-37 with manufacturing rights. They also procured one NA-47, copied it and produced their own version as the Watanabe K10W1. That occurred well before the Neutrality Act was created. The Japanese became proficient at copycat logic, adapting designs to their own tactical needs decades before WWII. After all, the North American Aviation Texan was "as good as anyone can make 'em," so why reinvent the wheel? A colorful SNJ-1 instrument trainer shows off its plumage in flight. *USN/NA*

Chapter 3

Churning, Burning, and Learning

At precisely 0750 hours on the clock – Hawaiian time – on the morning of December 7, 1941, the Imperial Japanese Navy (IJN) had launched their intended 'Sunday Punch' attack against the United States of America's great naval and army installations at Pearl Harbor, Territory of Hawaii.

Without any aid from the powerful Japanese Army, the IJN alone left the island of Oahu with the U.S. Army and Navy ships, aircraft, facilities and personnel churning and burning. Almost concurrently, Japan's army and naval forces were mutilating Manila while turning the military and naval installations and weapons in the Philippines into an identical condition.

If the top officials in this nation believed we were prepared for the type of war already demonstrated during the decade of the 1930s by German, Italian and Japanese, political aspirations, a 1920s mentality, a complete lack of knowledge or understanding of totalitarianism, or the plague of Isolationism must have isolated them from the realities of life. Mankind seems to have an inherent failure to understand the minds of power-mad imperialists.

In January 1939, Maj. Gen. Frank M. Andrews, then Chief of the GHQ Air Force – the fighting arm of the Army Air Corps – warned publicly that America only had a fifth- or even sixth-rate air power. His command had barely 400 first-line fighting planes, and who would have been in a better position to know that. For his efforts, General Andrews was replaced forthwith. (Of interest is the fact that in 1941 – not including December 7 casualties – the Army Air Force in the Hawaiian Islands alone had to write off at last 50 first-line combat aircraft as the result of accidents. Additionally, about half that number of AAF warplanes were out of service for varying periods while repairs were completed.)

Two things had become evident in Japan, at least to aviation journalists of the stature of Cy Caldwell at Aero Digest magazine: Expansion into the colonial territories of France, England and the Netherlands was a foregone conclusion by 1940. Secondly, interference by Uncle Sam and John Bull in these schemes would not be tolerated, even if it meant war. After all, there would be nothing to fear from the British, French or Dutch considering the situation that existed in Continental Europe by that summer.

Many very high-level authorities in Washington believed that the US fleet in the Pacific could handle any situation that might arise. Others were far more aware that the state of readiness of our navy, after years of neglect, was a myth. President Roosevelt was the first Chief of the Armed Forces since World War I to obtain authorization and funding to build battleships, new and efficient aircraft carriers and the necessary supporting warships. So, why wasn't the fleet ready? Mainly it was because it took years to design and build an aircraft carrier or a battleship. Our elected politicians scoffed at any suggestion about Japanese capabilities and nobody raised an eyebrow when it had to be known that Japan was ignoring the constraints of the Washington Naval Treaty. So was Germany. Realists know that treaties are made to be broken. The Army could never defend the Hawaiian Islands from an invasion under any of the then current conditions, and the Air Corps was in fractionally better shape. How could it have been otherwise?

It is important to point out that our first-line bomber force in 1940 consisted mainly of plodding Douglas B-18 and B-18A bombers and a handful of assorted Boeing B-17 models. First-line fighters consisted almost entirely of something less than 77 Seversky P-35s and fewer than 200 new Curtiss P-36s, each equipped with two machine guns. Germany and Great Britain, at the same time, had multi-gun fighters, and that armament included cannons up to 30mm. A B-18A bomber was "defended" with three or four .30-cal. machine guns, not one of which was in a power turret. No wonder General Andrews felt compelled to speak out.

Obviously the Japanese were not intending in any way to precede their attack with a formal declaration of war. They had paid strict attention to the performance of their pact ally, Nazi Germany, in dealing with Poland and Russia. General George Marshall, in his top-level staff position as military advisor to the president, was certainly privy to the highest level of intelligence information. In many ways, Japan had actually "telegraphed" their intentions about intolerance of British and American sanctions. The entire U.S. military and naval establishments should have been on highest alert status weeks before December 7, 1941.

Washington obviously learned nothing from the actions of Germany, Italy, and Japan in their aggression actions.

A week before the Pearl Harbor raid, the Honolulu Advertiser – a major newspaper in Hawaii – had blaring headlines about the expectation of an attack by Japan. The War Department's reaction was on the verge of being totally passive. At Wheeler Field on Oahu Island, a few short miles from the city, where most of the 87 Curtiss P-40B pursuit planes in Hawaii were based, those defensive fighters and a smaller number of obsolete Curtiss P-36s, blared out that passivity was rampant. Totally disregarding Axis nation modus operandi already demonstrated by the Germans in connection with Czechoslovakia and by the Japanese in China and Manchuria, the defensive actions taken were extremely naive. Contrary to all logic, the pursuit planes were lined up wingtip-to-wingtip, *drained* of fuel and *stripped* of ammunition! All this centered on taking precautions against sabotage…which could easily have been dealt with in other available ways. Why? The American public will never, ever know the absolute truth, of course. Logic tells you that you should read between the lines (noting the similarity to the word lies). All logical storm warnings were taken down. Most of the Army and Navy officer and enlisted staff treated Friday and Saturday nights as solid peacetime hours for relaxation and entertainment. Late at night, it was "lights out" as usual or partying all night.

In the states, at the U.S. Capital, White House and the Navy Department, a significant, multi-part document of Japanese intentions as transmitted to that nation's envoys in Washington was being decoded at a snail's pace by the Japanese embassy officials. Not far away, Navy cryptologists had decoded the document before the Japanese envoys were close to accomplishing their chore. Indeed, Gen. Marshall and the President were already aware of the message content about two hours before the massive IJN fleet of armed aircraft struck their mid-Pacific target.

A routine coded message sent by Marshall's office to Hawaii, Panama and the Philippines – inexplicably sent via commercial Western Union/RCA telegraph channels to those USN and U.S. Army headquarters – would have rung alarm bells all over the Hawaiian Islands and the other commands. It should have been sent via navy and military radio, teletype, telegraph or telephone – even uncoded in the clear – with the admonition that "This is Not an exercise." In that simple action alone, perhaps the Japanese would have called off the raid, knowing that all headquarters in Hawaii had been alerted for action. Even worse at the time, Gen. Marshall had arrived late for his meeting, eventually was talked into 'scrawling out' a note for transmittal of a "less than urgent" warning. There was virtually no time left before the Japanese raid was actually launched; yet Marshall himself seemed almost indifferent. Amazingly, even the Hawaiian Islands were to be alerted *after* MacArthur in the Philippines and Panama. Marshall even admitted that in later testimony! Use of the telephone in a scrambled message was lightly considered but rejected because some officers showed little confidence in the scrambler. That raises the question: Why was the scrambler situation left to indifferent corrective action? Why wasn't a person of Marshall's rank, stature and command responsibility more reactive? As Truman once put it, "The buck stops here." If so many underlings were alarmed by what they all seemed to know, why was the general acting as if he had no realistic reason to believe all of the flashing alarm signals?[4] Any lesser person who was responsible for so many lives ultimately lost would have faced a firing squad. Truman himself, later in life fired Gen. MacArthur with far less cause. Ultimately, well after the Japanese deed was done, courts martial trials proceeded, aimed at placing the blame. Of course that blame did not fall on the Secretary of War, Secretary of the Navy, Army Chief of Staff or the Chief of Naval Operations. Or upon the President. We will probably never know the truths.

Fortunately the American people responded to the Axis nations' actions against the U.S.A.'s national desire to settle problems peacefully with a far greater dedication of purpose than ever seen on this Continent since the American Revolution. The infant Arsenal of Democracy grew to maturity in one great hurry to help defeat nations intent on world domination. The lesson had been learned in the same general manner in which one might have gained the attention of a mule. As President Franklin D. Roosevelt stated before Congress in special session not many hours after Hawaii and the Philippine Islands were assaulted, December 7, 1941 " was a day that will live in infamy." Probably a good deal of introspection on the part of those at the top levels would have been in order before we were subjected to such disaster. (There are those who will view these statements as "revisionist" interpretations. That would be incorrect for two reasons. First, I can understand President Roosevelt's frustration with Isolationists who were not privy to guarded information and, indeed, he probably did need a logical reason for permitting a grievous act against America. I would estimate that with available intelligence information from all sources and our overall lack of understanding of the Oriental mind from every corner, he could hardly be blamed for not being an alarmist. As Gordon Prange has stated: "While the Pearl Harbor attack united the American people, it was too much to ask that unity in the war effort would also create political unity." Recall that Great Britain's Prime Minister Chamberlain blatantly chose to ignore every act of Hitler's Nazi takeovers and modus operandi, acting from weakness as if turning the other cheek would accomplish wonders. Perhaps worse, he gave the British citizenry false hope by acting enthusiastically and with his words. He lived a lie. What do they teach at Eton? The French military leaders evidently believed they had won World War I. Old, obsolete generals with a Maginot Line sense of security simply dissolved in the face of modern Teutonic military aggressiveness. Few seemed to have learned anything from years of stalemate and daily annihilation of thousands of "cannon fodder" troops at the order of incompetent leadership in WWI. And it is axiomatic that civil populations classically forget the horrors of war within weeks of an ending. The old "ounce of prevention is worth a pound of cure" thoughts disappear overnight. Even a new millennium has not corrected that trend.

Another point in my views about Roosevelt is that without his ability to convince Congress of an all-but-forgotten need for battleships and aircraft carriers, even in uneasy peacetime, our first line of defense would have been hopelessly crippled in fighting the Japanese. No other president since WWI showed even the slightest interest in military preparedness. Most were willing to let such things be ignored in the interests of getting re-elected. History always repeats its errors. But for his initiative regarding the 50,000 planes issue in May 1940, America would not have had a clear running start on aircraft production to the degree that existed on Dec. 7, 1941.

It was President Warren G. Harding who called for (and really wanted) the International Conference on Limitations of Armaments in 1921-22. The Washington Naval Treaty was generated during his term of office, but the USN did manage to obtain authorization to convert two incomplete battle cruiser hulls into the aircraft carriers U.S.S. *Lexington* (CV-2) and U.S.S. *Saratoga* (CV-3), mainly because by treaty they could not be completed for the original role. When Harding died, his vice president, Calvin Coolidge, succeeded to the presidency on 2 August 1923. He finished that term and was re-elected as president in 1924. Herbert Hoover was elected president in 1928 and the stock market crashed less than a year later. Hoover flatly opposed federal aid to the unemployed. He was defeated for re-election in 1932 by FDR. Roosevelt became the first president since World War I to order any new battleships (*North Carolina* and *Washington*) in 1937. He also managed to have no fewer than fifteen additional battleships ordered from 1938 to 1940. All but five of those were commissioned during the war years.

Our other World War I battleships underwent partial modernization in the 1930s, but all were limited to less than 35,000 tons by the Treaty. Even the two battleships ordered in 1937 did not exceed the limits imposed although other nations were failing to observe the terms. One small aircraft carrier, at a mere 14,500 tons, was ordered under Hoover's presidency a year after the market crash. Had he been re-elected, his attitude would have assured everyone than no additional carriers or battleships would have even been ordered during his term of office. America would not have had its planned Two-Ocean Navy, even if Roosevelt had been elected for the first time in 1936. Under no circumstances – in that scenario – could America have had even the *Yorktown* and *Enterprise* because it took four long years between the order date and the commissioning date. Even then months-long shakedown cruises are required to make the ship fit for war. We might have had two new battleships, the *North Carolina* and the *Washington* under the same election scenario, but there is no guarantee that would have occurred. Therefore, we would have had battleships, all ordered between 1909 and 1917! And little modernization could have been expected in the Depression years.

Those are the facts of life, and no other "pie-in-the-sky" script would be anything but fantasy. (Despite this author's politics, I am totally glad that we had a sensible man for president in those dark, dark days of 1930-1940.)

Our brave soldiers, sailors, marines and aviators fought back with serious limitations at Guadalcanal, Wake, Midway, and the Aleutians and in great sea/air

> Where, you might logically ask, did all this enlightened knowledge come from? Books, movies and TV programs generated in the last quarter century from people who hardly know what World War II was all about?? Not at all!! Both my father and I were active participants in WWII. He was deeply involved even before Dec. 7, 1941, as a senior advisor in William Knudsen's Office of Production Management (OPM). Once the production juggernaut was rolling, he was in command of USAAF Air Service Command groups, stateside and overseas (again). I was involved in the defense industry until entering the USAAF. The experience served me well. But long before WWII, I was a serious student of armaments, military actions worldwide, and military history. The main criteria for understanding: Paying attention to what was happening and what had occurred all through history. There is nothing more educational than participation. You cannot help but learn from experience.

battles in 1942 against terrific odds. In the summer of that same year, with the imagination and brilliance of several men, for the first time in history the mass aircraft ferrying operation of bombers, twin-engine transports and at least a full group of first-line fighters (P-38s) across the Atlantic Ocean to the U.K. was accomplished with great success. It was called Operation BOLERO. Later in that same year, many of the same aircraft joined in the successful Operation TORCH (the invasion of North Africa). Our Army Air Force became the key to the air defense of Australia and Southwest Pacific Islands. At home, American industry was beginning to roar. Entire new aircraft and engine plants such as Ford's Willow Run Bomber Plant and Consolidated's Fort Worth B-24 factory were constructed and began hammering out long-ranging 4-engine bombers. Jigs and fixtures created at Willow Run were fabulous compared to those encountered at Douglas' Santa Monica old-line factory complex. New tanks were designed and produced in places like Chrysler's state-of-the-art tank arsenal. Shipyards found radically different ways to construct freighters, warships and landing craft. Locomotives were soon in relatively mass production compared to pre-war methods.

[4]For a wonderful investigative report at the end of a 37-year investigation, see *AT DAWN WE SLEPT* by Gordon W. Prange, a man with outstanding insider credentials!

Often forgotten in referring to America's Arsenal of Democracy concentration on the mechanical products is the fact that the Arsenal also consisted of a huge training program for much needed manpower. One thing lacking on January 1, 1940, was even a trained cadre of multi-engine rated pilots. There was no great pool of such young men, but suddenly factories started to rumble in manufacturing twin-engine fighters, bombers and transports plus a flock of new four-engine bombers and transports. It is necessary to recall that in the late 1930s, Douglas Aircraft (a major aircraft builder) had produced only a single DC-4X 4-engine airliner and one huge 4-engine bomber, the XB-19. Large multi-engine flying boats existed but were not commonplace. Crews were needed, and our arsenal provided the planes and means to train such crews. This picture of USN officers was probably generated in connection with a pre-Pearl Harbor recruiting program for pilot training, but we are fairly certain it was taken sometime in 1941. The Vought-Sikorsky OS2U-1 in the background lends a nice touch, especially since many were assigned to training duties at Pensacola, Florida, the site of this picture, we presume. Dress uniforms and flying togs are emphasized. It is also a fitting and appropriate introduction to the next chapter which is heavily oriented toward the training equipment and programs created hurriedly as the probability of war involvement loomed. *USN via NA*

BELOW   One of the first-wave defense plants built under the president's 50,000 Airplanes a Year plan was the Martin Middle River (MD.) Plant #2. It was government financed, but it was not one of the "Blackout" factories built in such large numbers during the war. Shown here are many of the earliest B-26s (no suffix letter) which soon found their way to Langley Field, VA., with most going into war activity immediately after Pearl Harbor was attacked. Although the Martin B-26 (Model 179) won the design competition by a significant margin, the company did not get the full contract award of 385 airplanes. Martin conceded that it would not be able to deliver 385 bombers within 24 months as spelled out. They had a full-house contract for $44 million worth of Model 187 Baltimores on an Anglo-French order and they were manufacturing PBM patrol bombers for the USN. Once again the unanswered question about a second source for alternative Lockheed P-38s is spotlighted. A new large government-owned plant was authorized and constructed near Omaha, Nebraska, to build B-26 Marauders. Martin's main plant was in the Baltimore, Maryland, vicinity on the East Coast with no realistic chance of being attacked by air. But the government wanted the new plant built as a dispersed plant far from the coastline, seemingly forgetting that the sole source for P-38s was at Burbank, CA, only several minutes by air from the coast nearest to Japan. Also forgotten was the fact that no prototype B-26 or North American B-25 had been ordered for testing. Marauder early development problems were so serious that plans were afoot to cancel production of the B-26 bomber in 1943. What motivated some actions of the WPB?   *Glenn L. Martin Co*

ABOVE   It would be deceptive, or at least disingenuous, to say that all aircraft companies in the U.S.A. did their part to make this country proud of the part they played in making America the Arsenal of Democracy. Brewster Aeronautical Corp. was one of those incompetently managed companies. As an old-line carriage and custom auto body maker, Brewster incompetently operated was respected, but the stock market crash and Depression ended that. Like Grumman, BAC began, in 1932, to make aircraft floats and components. By 1934 the Navy was striving to make a transition to monoplane designs, awarding a contract for design and construction of a prototype dive bomber. By 1937, the resulting XSBA-1 appeared to offer enough attributes so that the Naval Aircraft Factory built thirty modified versions as the SBN-1s between November 1940 and March 1942. These were delivered to Bombing Squadron 3 (VB-3), later serving as trainers aboard USS *Hornet* (CV-8) for Torpedo Squadron 8 (VT-8). Using similar technology, Brewster produced a naval shipboard fighter, the XF2A-1 delivered to NAS Anacostia in December 1937. Navy BuAer ordered 54 developed versions as F2A-1s when Grumman's XF4F-2 design encountered extreme developmental problems. Brewster's F2A-1s were outdated as naval warplanes by events in Europe. When Russia attacked Finland, U.S. law permitted the transfer of 43 of the F2A-1 (B-239s) Navy fighters to the Finnish government. The Buffalos served well in that war. This B-339 with the NX tail markings had been ordered by the Belgian government, but with the overrun of that nation, 40 airplanes were delivered to the RAF in England. The British Purchasing Mission had also ordered 170 as B-339Es, then named Buffalo, for service the RAF, RAAF and RNZAF. Deliveries began in July 1940.   *Via Richard Starinchak*

It was not until after the first Douglas 7B flew as a "Christmas gift " in December 1938 that the French Purchasing Mission placed a production order for the light bomber. Moreover, their British peers did not participate in that procurement program. Soon, however, the British were flying DB-7 Bostons from contracts taken over after the astounding collapse of the Allied forces on the Continent. These early-series DB-7s were powered by P&W R-1830 Twin Wasp engines and had the smaller vertical empennage of the earlier 7B. Although the AAC tested two versions of the 7B (gun nose, bomber nose), no interest was shown. When interest was shown, it was in an A-20 (no suffix) version with Wright R-2600 turbo-supercharged engines. A top speed of 390 mph was demonstrated, but apparently the Cyclone 14 was not entirely compatible with turbosupercharging. All production A-20s were reworked to delete the GE units. Ultimately almost all became P-70's at the Santa Monica plant. No other Cyclone 14-powered production aircraft were equipped with turbosuperchargers. An evening view of the new Douglas Long Beach factory shows A-20 Havocs for the Air Corps at the final assembly stage.   *Douglas via Walter Boyne*

RIGHT & BELOW Senior officers in the Army Air Corps of the 1930s treated Major Alexander de Seversky rather badly although they really owed him a debt of gratitude. It was Seversky himself who demonstrated his SEV-3 monoplane at Wright Field and managed to show the Corps the error of their ways in basic training of pilots. Almost grudgingly, they awarded a contract for thirty all-metal low-wing BT-8 basic trainers to Seversky Aircraft in FY1935. Up to that time, for several years, they had converted obsolete observation biplanes or put bigger engines in primary trainers to create "basic trainers." The BT-8 had some tricky flight characteristics to master, but it put cadet training into the modern age by 1936. Newly reorganized North American Aviation created a new basic trainer, their NA-16, in time to compete in a 1935 competition for additional monoplane basic trainers where it was victorious over the BT-8 and a Curtiss-Wright CW-19. In a planned move to Southern California, corporate head "Dutch" Kindelberger managed to build a new factory at Inglewood, California, and still meet contractual requirements to fill the order for 42 new BT-9 monoplane trainers. Of course these new basic trainers were allocated to the new Army "West Point of the Air" at Randolph Field, Texas. On the flight line, the blue and yellow, striped-tail trainers presented a pretty picture. Seen in flight, a second-order BT-9A is seen posed against a cloud backdrop. *Fred Bamberger, USAAC*

Everyone realized that it would do no good to build 50,000 airplanes a year if there were not enough pilots to fly them, so programs for training were generated on a scale never even dreamed of since the Wright Brothers made their first flight. That meant that competent instructors were going to be needed in great numbers, many flying fields would be required, and there would be a huge need for mechanics. One good solution was to use existing and expanded civilian flight schools to provide primary training. North American's hopes for gaining a strong foothold in manufacturing primary trainers – using a derivative of the original NA-16 – did not work out as hoped for. In the meantime, they developed the AT-6 Texan as a Basic Combat type (the BC-1), soon reidentified as an Advanced Trainer. Nobody was about to come close to the success of the AT-6, so over a period of a few years the company manufactured thousands for the AAF and USN in several slightly different configurations. Not only that, they sold hundreds more to numerous foreign governments, especially Canada and Great Britain. In fact, total production of all models, with the AT-6 concept leading the way and including several training versions built under license, exceeded 20,000 airplanes. Vultee benefitted from that success by building thousands of their own design basic trainer, the BT-13 and BT-15. It could not have been as good a performaner as the NAA BT-14 was because it had 50 less horsepower. But with training airplanes like those, America was destined to turn out the best crop of pilots in huge numbers in the least amount of time.   *USAAF via Gerry Markgraf*

Without the impetus of war threats, American development of aircraft and associated equipment technology in the two decades between WWI and WWII meandered along at a relative snail's pace. At the end of the "War to end all wars," American fighters usually had but two cowl-mounted machine guns. When Curtiss P-40s were ordered en masse as the outcome of a 1939 pursuit competition, armament consisted of two synchronized machine guns. And that was already three years *after* young Lieutenant Ben Kelsey had specified four guns and a cannon for the P-38. So, two decades had passed with no real improvement in armament or oxygen systems in an anti-war nation. Douglas' El Segundo factory produced their 7B design prototype at the very end of 1938. France, lagging in design progress, ordered an improved version, developed rapidly in the face of a 105-plane order, and the DB-7 version took off on 17 August 1939. This Ed Heinemann-led design was soon ordered by the Air Corps, again rapidly improved into the A-20 with a maximum speed of nearly 350 mph with bombs loaded. The attack type it was replacing, the A-17A carried a far smaller bomb load externally, and in that condition could barely exceed 210 mph. Havocs did not get any faster in the next four years, but gross weight climbed by nearly 6,500 lbs.! In less than three years, Douglas' XA-26 was flying. Production A-26C Invaders could attain 370+ mph with nearly twice the range and at least 80 percent greater bomb loads. Firepower was also increased significantly. Redesignated as B-26s, the Invaders served well in the Korean War and in the much later war in Viet Nam. Here we have a rare Boeing-built Douglas A-20C. *Rudy Arnold via R. Starinchak*

Left over from the 1941 southern military maneuvers, a camouflaged North America O-47A seemed out of character like many original draftees who had expected to be going home after one single year in the military service. Their theme had been "Over the hill by....." Of course it never happened. Since the O-47A and B observation airplanes were more powerful and faster than the AAF's Northrop A-17 and A-17A attack aircraft – in case anybody even noticed – it would seem logical to have given them a more useful role. By eliminating the third crew member in all O-47s, replacing camera equipment with a heavy bomb in a belly recess and adding underwing bomb racks, O-47s could do more harm than any A-17.Heavy-caliber forward-firing machine guns could also have been added. Such was not even considered, but they did try fitting large twin float gear on one, a bulbous Boulton-Paul gun turret in another, and even a French-concept greenhouse-like observation station in the belly of a third O-47. *USAAF*

Lt. Fred Bamberger "commanded" the photography office at relatively new Randolph Field, despite being a rated pilot at a time when pilots were sorely needed, most likely attributable to his known history in color photography. It can be certain that Fred did not hide the facts from key people. (For that, we can all be thankful.) It did not take long for our cameraman to arrange for two North American BT-9s circling the round perimeter of Randolph while our colorful photographer snapped happily away with his private Contax 35 mm camera. Therefore, six decades or more later, we have the opportunity to view that septuagenarian Army Air Corps "West Point of the Air " base in the same colors it was viewed in by aviators of that time. Wartime training of officers, pilots, infantrymen, cannoneers, sailors, marines, and tankers had great priority to man America's arsenal. Life itself seemed to be running at double time. Randolph Field was a new $10,000,000 flight training center for the Army Air Corps, beginning operations as 1932 was just weeks away. Most likely, its creation was heavily inspired in the heady days following Charles Lindbergh's ocean venture. Most fortunately for all Americans, it was funded in the pre-Depression days. All flight training activity was to be relocated from Kelly Field to this massive base (at the time) as soon as it was completed and dedicated on 2 November 1931. Notice that all hangars were located on opposite sides of the central base, and there were no paved runways for heavy aircraft, few of which existed. It was a sod field. *Fred Bamberger*

Speeding down one of many new concrete runways, undoubtedly as a result of probably the largest airport building program in history, a twin-engine AT-9 advanced trainer, known as the Jeep, is seen about to lift off. Designed and built at Curtiss-Wright's plant near St. Louis, the airplane was looked upon as a short route to the training of multi-engine pilots scheduled to fly such high-performance aircraft as the Martin B-26, Douglas A-26, North American B-25 and, of course, the Lockheed P-38s. In that role, it suffered a checkered career. Some people would swear by it; others would swear at it. With engines set close together, relatively, and plenty of vertical fin and rudder area, it should have been reasonably safe. Many blamed its notorious reputation on the fact that it did not have feathering propellers. Why didn't that say the same things about the Beech AT-10 and AT-11 or the Cessna "Bamboo Bomber" AT-17? It is a fact that at the height of our involvement in WWII, AT-9s were taken out of service for a time. It is probably true that Curtiss-Wright Corp. turned out a moderately flawed design, but seemed unable to correct the flaws. C-W produced 791 of the so-called Jeep AT-9 trainers in two configurations, the AT-9A being slightly improved.

All things considered, it must have been a terribly bitter pill for Major Alexander Seversky (the de prefix having gone by the wayside) to swallow when the Republic XP-47B took off for the first time from Republic Airport on 6 May 1941. That signaled the start of a remarkably successful career as one of the world's best fighters. Major Seversky had been ousted as head of the company he had formed. While he was in Europe demonstrating the Seversky EP1-68 and 2PA-BX military aircraft, Wallace Kellett had become president of Seversky Aircraft Company by direction of financier Paul Moore. It was the old Judas Iscariot act. Seversky countered upon his return with a lawsuit. Under pressure from top echelons of the U.S. government, Republic Aviation became successor to Seversky. How did the XP-47B come into existence? It most certainly did *not* begin with a proposal from Republic. The initial requirements stemmed from studies by the Emmons Board led by M/Gen. Delos Emmons in 1940. Alexander Kartveli, VP at Republic, and a small retinue of officials attended an Air Corps Materiel Division specification meeting. The outgrowth was cancellation of the XP-47/XP-47A pursuit contract in favor of a new, powerful XP-47B, the direct outgrowth of the XP-44 interceptor design. It was actually a modification of those P-43 pursuit airplanes that stemmed directly from Major Seversky's AP-4 entry in the 1939 Pursuit Competition held at Wright Field, his own personal conception of what a modern fighter should be. Construction-wise, it was a parallel to the XP-41 modification of the P-35 but with advanced features. Foremost was the pioneering installation of a turbo supercharger in the aft section of the airframe. Although the major production contract outgrowth of that competition was for hundreds of Curtiss P-40s, a "runner up" award led directly to the Republic YP-43 Service Test Airplane contract for thirteen aircraft. The Major was out of the loop by then, but world conditions dictated that production of P-43 Lancers should continue, if for no other reason than to keep the Seversky-cum-Republic workforce intact. Needless to say, Kellett was not long for Farmingdale. *Republic*

Typical of the aircraft industry as a whole, Lockheed Aircraft Corporation was able to recruit many fine pilots to ferry their new aircraft to distribution points and to flight test production aircraft as they rolled from assembly lines. Even more-experienced pilots were there to accelerate testing of advanced-design aircraft. In operational service, all aircraft being flown without artificial time limits plus the rigors of combat environments would reveal various weaknesses. One famous pilot quickly hired by Lockheed for advanced flight test work was world girdling and distance-record pilot, Jimmy Mattern shown here with a P-38D. The Lightning shown was carrying extensive test equipment in place of the armament. Compare the rudimentary flight gear worn by the pilot, even to the elementary crash helmet. Oxygen equipment was not compatible in 1939-42 capabilities of the aircraft because war in Europe, especially during the Battle of Britain, found the aircraft battle arenas rising to altitudes exceeding the target levels of military planners of the 1930s. Without pressurized breathing equipment or pressure cabins, the dangers above 32,000 feet were fast becoming threats to life. Anoxia would bring on the threat of creeping drowsiness, and aeroembolism, for example, was a more serious threat. Above 35,000 feet, even a few seconds of oxygen deprivation could cause blood to boil. Motion pictures ("movies") such as *Test Pilot* and *Dive Bomber* of the 1939-41 era delved into the aeromedical sciences rapidly becoming evident. Lockheed test pilot Marshall Headle had his career potential and his life cut short by a malfunction in the company's pioneering pressure test chamber. Venturing to attainable altitudes without new, properly developed oxygen systems – a lower priority in the U.S.A. behind overseas requirements in early 1942 – could result in death without warning. *Eric Miller-LAC*

Virtually everybody had a "home grown" camouflage scheme in WWII, and there were frequent changes because of the learning curve and radical changes attributable to the terrain associated with varying combat theaters of operation. The accompanying photo of a British RAF Kittyhawk (H81-A) illustrates how well one British scheme makes the aircraft blend with farm field backgrounds. Over water or desert areas, the effectiveness was not nearly as great. Early Curtiss P-40/H81-B Tomahawk fighters were essentially Curtiss H75 Mohawk/AAC P-36 airframes fitted with Allison C-series inline engines, and they usually did not have bullet-proof glass for windshields or self-sealing fuel tanks nor armor protection. Evolutionary changes brought on by lessons learned by the British in the heat of combat were integrated as fast as possible, with the greatest changes creating the P-40D/export H87-A models, renamed as Kittyhawks. These all had a new F-series Allison V-1710 engine featuring a new, shorter and tougher reduction gear case with external-spur gear, significantly altering the nose shape and gun locations. British purchases and the American Lend-Lease program resulted in foreign Allies receiving some 2,992 Kittyhawks, primarily going to the United Kingdom. America had been unwilling to fund the development of fighters, bombers, aircraft engines and naval aircraft of advanced design during the Depression/Isolationist years of the mid-1930s period. Curtiss' P-40/Tomahawk airframe was at least 3-4 years behind the Germans and British in fighters at the end of the '30s decade, but probably this nation was on a par or better track in heavy bomber evolution, thanks to the Boeing Airplane Co. As the late B/Gen. Ben Kelsey has stated, our aircraft weaponry was essentially back at 1918 levels because senior ordnance decision makers could not understand why those "Air Corps boys could not be satisfied with what was available." It appears that the biggest advantage Americans enjoyed was the well-trained pool of pilots, navigators, bombardiers and gunners as early as December 7, 1941, coupled with a massive wealth of natural resources and our manufacturing base. *Jack Kerr via Warren Thompson*

These two photographs of the Northrop N-1M flying wing must be the rarest of such pictures this writer has ever encountered. This is the modified N-1M featuring revised sweepback angle and zero anhedral on the wingtips, usually seen in photographs of the N-1M. As viewed here, the airplane is nearly a pure flying wing. The fact that it had no computers to control flight is just as remarkable. One would suspect that the airplane, with no vertical fin stabilization, would have shown a tendency to precess (pivot) about its vertical center in the same way that the XB-35 and XB-49 were reported to have behaved during simulated bombing runs. The modified N-1M was relatively stable in level flight, and that was confirmed by the final design of the N-9M aircraft that followed. Unlike the later research flying wings, the N-1M was created as a variable geometry aircraft. On the ground only, technicians could vary the tip anhedral/dihedral, the dihedral of the outboard main wing panels, and the sweepback of those same panels by as much as 15 degrees. As originally constructed, the N-1M was powered by two 65 hp Lycoming O-145 aircooled engines. Maximum altitude attainable with those engines and with no passenger aboard, was about 15 feet! Actually if was then flying on ground cushion effect! Those little 4-cylinder engines were replaced with a pair of 6-cylinder Franklin 6AC-264F2 aircooled engines rated at 120 hp each. With about 240 hp available, the airplane performed its tasks without any real difficulties, even with one dead unit on Army Hot Day conditions while operating from Muroc Army Air Base, essentially a dry lake bed.   *Via Gerald Balzer*

Intensive flight testing of thirteen uncamouflaged YP-38 Service Test aircraft was conducted by Lockheed in California, Air Materiel Command at Wright and Patterson Fields Ohio, and at Selfridge Field, Michigan over a period of many months. One YP-38 was even installed in the NACA full-size wind tunnel at Langley Field, Virginia. Cannon firing tests were conducted at Oscoda, Michigan. The program actually amounted to initiation of what became known as Accelerated Flight Testing as the war rolled on. Unfortunately, Lockheed test pilot Ralph Virden, at the controls of this airplane pictured, was killed just days later when he became a bit overzealous in a testing program. Thousands of Lockheed workers were listening to some patriotic speechmaking by visiting VIPs. It was a beautiful day, noontime, and the crowd gathered outside on Lockheed Air Terminal property. Virden finished his testing of a spring tab assembly on the elevator with a typical – for Virden – dive acceleration to near ground level before pulling out. This was contrary to all instructions to him. A part broke, snapping that large elevator surface fully upward. The design stress limits were exceeded by far, breaking the entire empennage away from the tail booms. The airplane crashed into a bungalow in Glendale in an inverted position. Virden must have died instantly. Incidentally, that death led directly to Anthony "Tony" LeVier's induction into designer Kelly Johnson's experimental flight test unit, supervised by noted aerobatics pilot Milo Burcham.   *Lockheed/Author's Coll.*

ABOVE and OVERLEAF TOP   It was semi-affectionately referred to as "The Yellow Peril" by men of various ranks in the navy. Revealing its beginnings dating back to the Depression-spawned NRA (National Recovery Act) of the period (1934), the design and prototype for this naval primary trainer possibly may have owed much to "make work" politics. It was a typically rugged, simple biplane design intended for operations interchangeably as a landplane and seaplane. Perhaps another reason for creating the trainer, other than a basic need for a newer design than the 1920s type already aging rapidly, was to use up a huge inventory of Wright J-5 engines, out of production since 1929. Whatever the reasons might have been, the prototype was first flown in 1935 at the Naval Aircraft Factory, Philadelphia. Official identity of the primary trainer was XN3N-1. A simple, rugged single central float plus twin auxiliary floats at the wingtips were readily interchangeable with the fixed landing gear used for operation from land. Between June 1936 and 1938, the NAF delivered 179 production N3N-1s. This version of the trainer generally had a so-called Townsend ring cowling for the aircooled radial engine. A subsequent order for improved or simplified N3N-3 versions resulted in delivery of 816 additional airplanes, but the cowling feature was eliminated. Thousands of naval aviation cadets received their primary training on N3Ns during WWII. Although most of these "Yellow Perils" were declared surplus when that war ended, a handful remained in use at Annapolis, Md, the U.S. Naval Academy as part of the midshipmen's curriculum. The N3N-3s were finally retired in 1961. No. 15 shown was a USMC glider-towing aircraft used in the training program at Page Field, SC.   *James Sullivan Coll.*

Glider flight training was adopted on a relatively modest scale in pre-Pearl Harbor days to aid in the indoctrination of recruits who could be considered for flight training. As such, the Marine Corps had six Schweizer LNS-1 gliders operating from the Parris Island training camp airfield, MCAS Page Field, SC. These aircraft were essentially trainer adaptations of civil aviation Schweizer sailplanes. At Page Field, the LNS-1 gliders were usually towed to launch altitude by one of the N3N trainers. *USN via Author*

The next step up from flying primary trainers – more often than not, biplanes – was generally movement into more powerful all-metal monoplane basic trainers. At that stage the neophyte pilot had double or triple the horsepower at his command, and he had to learn how to cope with it. This Vultee BT-13 Valiant, often referred to as the "Vibrator" in WWII days, was one of the earliest batch delivered in 1940 and carrying a complete pre-war paint scheme. Streamlined landing gear fairings were soon treated as excess baggage and were dispensed with. USN version was designated SNV-1.   *AAF Training Command/Robert Archer*

OPPOSITE   To those men in cadet training, being launched into space aboard a float-equipped biplane in the first half of the 20th century it was akin to being shot from a cannon at the circus. Moving from zero to flying speed with virtually no loss in altitude while still maintaining self-composure had to be exciting. In those days before Pearl Harbor, the favored single-float (vs. two main floats) Vought O3U-3 Corsair was a favorite for such catapulting. The standard shipboard catapult used at Pensacola was charged with gunpowder cells, providing instant departure. Of course the launching cradle was arrested at the end of the catapult, with the aircraft sailing off into space over water. Scout/Observation Vought Corsairs began serving aboard carriers, on battleships and cruisers, and from shore bases in 1927. Although most of the Corsairs were delivered as observation airplanes, many were redesignated as VS (scout) airplanes in service, a category change not well understood by "landlubber" persons. Generally, Curtiss SOC Seagull series aircraft, also being biplanes, revealed a combined function in their scout-observation designations as they took the place of Corsairs. As 1941 came to an upsetting end, there were still 141 Corsair biplanes operating from various USN air stations, aerodynamically little changed from the 1926 prototype. In all those years, horsepower had only increased from 450 to 550, and even the Curtiss Seagulls could only boast of 600 horsepower. Float-equipped Corsairs still had useful lives at Pensacola in their training roles. In WWII, Vought-Sikorsky OS2U Kingfisher monoplanes took over most of the first-line operational status for observation/scout duties. A competitive (?) Curtiss SO3C Seamew type was ordered in quantity, but it proved to be a dismal failure despite major attempts to correct its inherent faults. Seamews were just one more catastrophic failure of the money-grubbing top management at Curtiss-Wright Corporation headquarters, a sad commentary on the good work done earlier by Glenn Curtiss and his workers. This catapult launch sequence of a VN-2D squadron Vought O3U-3 at Pensacola in 1941 provides a nice trip down memory lane.   *USN/NA (3)*

ABOVE   Well, God bless the women of America, at least. When more than 16 million men were called to war, including a very large percentage of the younger, able-bodied men, women flocked to the rescue to fill business and industry gaps. More than five million strong, they helped build aircraft, tanks, warships and Liberty ships; they also kept the economy under control by working in the offices of every government agency and all industry. Most surprising was their ability to do a large part of the heavy-duty jobs such as overhauling locomotives, buses and trucks. Not only that, the Army had thousands of WACs (Womens' Army Corps). WAVES (*W*omen *A*ppointed for *V*oluntary *E*mergency *S*ervice), Lady Marines and WASPs (Women Airforce Service Pilot), those wonderful female AAF pilots who ferried every type of military airplane – usually from the manufacturer to any destination where they were needed without delay. Aviatrix Jackie Cochran used her knowledge of flying and her record-breaking fame to 'bulldoze' AAF kingpins into creating a niche where women pilots could serve their country best. The WAVE pictured herewith was assigned as a mechanic at NAS Pensacola and is standing on the wing of a North American SNJ advanced trainer.   *USN/NA*

2.) ACCELERATION

3.) UP, UP, AND AWAY !

**1.) LOADING ON THE
       CATAPULT**

Vought O3U-3 Corsair

BELOW Just imagine being a model airplane builder, aviation magazine reader and then Naval Aviation Cadet at Corpus Christi, TX, after Pearl Harbor and being able to solo in a fat, old Grumman F3F-3. You might never want to leave that duty assignment. That red off-shade cowling and the colorful prop tips just add to the pleasure. At least Cadet Thanas had that "awful" assignment. Few would deny that if naval pilots in Brewster F2As had fought against the Mitsubishi A6M2 Model 21 that appeared at Pearl Harbor on December 7, 1941, the results might have been worse than meetings between the Japanese planes and the Grumman biplanes. What the F3F-2 and -3 airplanes lacked in fighting performance, they made up in for it in charm and maneuverability. But that is not a happy balance of power in the life of a fighter pilot. *L. of C.*

ABOVE This author and USAAF glider training arrived in California nearly in a dead heat (an appropriate statement) in the weeks following immediately after the war between America and Japan became reality. California's desert areas were, in most cases, probably as trackless and treeless as any African desert. For several reasons, the AAF chose to create their glider training base at a pathetically boring site called Twentynine Palms. Of course that makes a liar out of me because I said there were no trees. Palms are not great shade trees. (Also, the Joshua Tree National Monument close by has trees that cast no shade at all at high noon.) In those days, the desert town of Palm Springs was hardly more than a real estate development conjured up by Mary Pickford's actor-husband Buddy Rogers. It was a place for the rich and famous to escape the madding crowds of fanatical fans. Automobiles mostly lacked any form of air-conditioning, and cool drinking water was generally at a premium in that vast desert country. The terrain and the heat most likely generated enough thermals to fly every glider known to man. Accelerated procurement allowed the AAF to have perhaps 154 Laister-Kauffman TG-4 type gliders in hand, and apparently most of them were assembled at 29 Palms. If the one main hangar was new, it looked old in pictures. There is probably no end to the list of obsolete and obsolescent airplanes that could have been utilized for glider towing purposes, including civilian types that could have been or were drafted into military service. More than likely, although source information is scarce, the large inventory of Stearman PT-13 biplane primary trainers offered several opportunities for the mild conversion to such duty. For the AAF, this training program did not start any too soon. Within two and a half years, hundreds of qualified glider pilots were needed for invasion of *Festung Europa* operations.   *AAF*

ABOVE   New primary training cadets were introduced for the first time to their new "make or break" training airplanes at Corpus Christi, Texas, hundreds of times during WWII in scenes akin to this one. Spotted on the concrete pad is a Stearman N2S trainer with an instructor and students discussing the schedule and syllabus for the day. In the general background, NAF N3Ns, manufactured by the government's Naval Aircraft Factory, shared the spotlight with the Stearmans (manufactured by the Stearman Division of Boeing Airplane Co. in Wichita, Kansas). Although a new Stearman X70 airplane won an Air Corps competition in 1934, the U.S. Navy BuAer was the first to procure these new trainers under the designation NS-1 (Stearman Model 73). The steel tube, fabric-covered biplanes were improved and basically standardized in 1936 with 220-hp Lycoming radial engines, and all new versions were to be Model 75s. These rugged trainers served the USN and AAF well throughout WWII. Something over 8000 Stearman Kaydet trainers were built for the two major services during WWII.   *USN/NA*

LEFT   Here is a man, proud to be a Chief Aviation Pilot. In peacetime and on into wartime a penny-pinching Congress was just a nuisance because President Roosevelt always seemed to find a way around or through them. Part of the real nuisance was the Navy's own budget bureau. Requests for needed money did not even get past these people to be considered by Congress. Apparently a couple of congressional acts pertaining mainly to naval aircraft procurement (or authorization might be more to the point) authorized expanding the enlisted pilot situation to one where there were Chief and First Class Aviation Pilots. (Officers were classed as Naval Aviators.) Ultimately the situation boiled down to the fact that enlisted aviation pilots would constitute 30 percent of all flying personnel. According to figures which boggle the mind, naval reserve pilots did not number 200 in the U.S.A., even at a time when it was quite evident to most personnel that the country would be at war sooner rather than later. Naval budgetary people, pacifists, isolationists and congressmen were some of our worst enemies. While it is perhaps understandable that naval aircraft strength fell from a very high level to less than 1000 aircraft in the mid 1930s, that strength – a ridiculous term under the circumstances – had only grown to about 2000 aircraft of all types in **1938!** One great miracle of the Arsenal was the ability to provide the structural facilities and infrastructure to support the training of thousands of pilots and maintenance personnel.   *USN/NA*

In the summer of 1940, the USS *Saratoga*, USS *Yorktown*, and USS *Enterprise* were assigned to two aircraft carrier divisions in the Pacific Fleet. Their offensive weapons in 1937 consisted of several new squadrons of Curtiss SBC-3 Helldiver biplanes, replacing obsolete Vought SBU-1s[5]. As, exposed previously, these new dive bombers were developed hurriedly in 1935 when the parasol-winged Curtiss XSBC-1 (BuNo. 9225) was destroyed in a second crash. Mysteriously, the same BuNo. was painted on the completely redesigned XSBC-2 biplane that had a new P&W R-1535 engine in a new cowling. Even the propeller was new. Production versions appeared in USN squadrons by 1937, designated as SBC-3s. The final SBC-3 was refitted with a new Wright R-1820 and promptly redesignated XSBC-4. That single-row radial R-1820 supposedly developed 950 horsepower, up about 200 hp from the engines in SBC-3s. Our fleets may have had new aircraft carriers, but even in June 1938 and later the USS *Lexington* and USS *Ranger* had the 1932-design SBU-1s as their offensive weaponry, again assigned to VS scouting squadrons. The more powerful SBC-4s joined some fleet squadrons in 1939. Totally unknown to fleet commanders was the fact that IJN aircraft carriers were being equipped with new Nakajima monoplane torpedo bombers (dual role) and monoplane dive bombers resembling our own Air Corps Northrop A-17 attack planes. In other words, our largest and most powerful military aircraft producer could not provide planes to match Japan's supposedly obsolete and "copycat" types. The hidebound Bureau of Aeronautics specifications evidently reflected caterpillar-speed design progress. What was the Office of Naval Intelligence (ONI) doing, or did the highest ranking fleet admirals dismiss ONI reports as "impossible"? One of those two possibilities was a probability.   *R. Starinchak from USN*

[5] Any person who had worked on any kind of aircraft would see that Curtiss Airplane Company's ruse tying the SBC-3 to the XSBC-1 should have been detected immediately. Powerplant, fuselage, tail and wings were absolutely far from matching any part of the XSBC-1. Only the nameplate had survived the final crash of the XSBC-1.

Hardly aided by financial conditions in the midst of the Depression, the U.S. Navy was driven to make the painful transition from the slow-landing biplane to faster monoplanes. Among the first to join the fleets were dive bombers and torpedo bombers, with the former given a dual role as scouts. Chance Vought in the east produced the rather handsome SB2U-1 while Northrop in the west turned out the BT-1 dive bomber with partially retractable landing gear. Production BT-1s were built in the former Moreland truck factory in El Segundo, Calif., just across the highway from Mines Field (now Los Angeles International Airport). The 54 unspectacular BT-1s ordered by the USN were carrier-based, assigned to Bombing Five (VB-5) as deliveries began in 1938. One BT-1 was converted as the prototype XBT-2 with a version of the flush inboard-retracting landing gear developed for the Northrop 3-A fighter. An engine change to the Wright XR-1820-32 Cyclone, projected to develop 1,000 hp very soon, proved to be a wise move. Major stockholder Douglas Aircraft changed the Northrop status to the Douglas El Segundo Division, April 1937. Further redesign of the XBT-2 resulted in the SBD-1, with an initial 1939 order for 57 examples for the Marine Corps to be distributed to bombing squadrons VMB-1 and VMB-2. On the same date, an improved SBD-2 version was ordered for Navy squadrons VB-2, VB-6 and VS-6 for duty on the USS *Lexington*

and USS *Enterprise* in late 1941. An SBD-3 Dauntless assigned to VS-41 is shown about to trap aboard the USS *Ranger* (CV4) during transitional training exercises in September 1942. Within two months they were in combat as participants in OPERATION TORCH in North Africa. Out of all the AAF and Navy aircraft committed to the Battle of Midway just three months earlier, it is safe to say that Douglas Dauntless dive bombers were the only successful attackers of the battle and Grumman F4F Wildcats the only successful defenders. The highly touted Norden bombsights in Boeing B-17Es were absolutely useless against maneuvering warships. *USN/NA*

If Douglas Dauntlesses proved to be winners under the SBD Navy identifications in the Battle of Midway, they were unwanted and unloved when wearing an Army Air Force uniform. They were just not up to the job that had to be done. Other than having the arresting gear deleted and a pneumatic tailwheel tire in place of the Navy version's hard rubber wheel, the A-24s were essentially clones of the SBDs. It did not take long for General George C. Kenney – assigned to take command of the Allied Air Forces in the Southwest Pacific and the Fifth Air Force in August 1942 – to conclude that the Douglas AAF A-24s serving in the 3rd Light Bombardment (Dive) squadron were essentially useless for the job assignment. They were dead slow at 250 mph tops, short ranged, and vulnerable aircraft. A typical A-24 Dauntless is shown in flight. Kenney wanted P-38s and P-47s, neither of which were popular at the time with the 8th Air Force. He badgered General H.H. Arnold to get such aircraft, but with his personal salesmanship gifts. He made it clear that he certainly did not want more A-24s. When he replaced Lt. Gen. George Brett, the latter was not getting the job done in the Southwest Pacific arena. Kenney proved to be *the* major factor in the turnaround in the situations in that operational area. *AAF via Robt. D. Archer*

Once America was drawn – actually clubbed – into the war, hundreds of aircraft destined for shipment to England were commandeered by the U.S. government. One type available in significant numbers was the Lockheed Hudson Mk.III in various configurations. This particular version, cloaked in typical British camouflage paints, had the RAF roundels painted over. It was redesignated A-29-LO. Typically, the British serial number remained in the normal locations and no attempt was made to provide USAAF tail numbers. All of this evidently took place at the "scene of the crime," Floyd Bennett Field, NY, also known during the war as NAS New York. Thousands of aircraft were ferried from or prepared for shipment overseas at Floyd Bennett Field, named for a pilot on RAdm. Richard Byrd's pioneering flight over the North Pole in 1926. Bennett was awarded the Congressional Medal of Honor. Other important departure points in the area were nearby NAF Roosevelt Field and Newark Airport, NJ. Roosevelt Field was named in honor of former President Theodore Roosevelt's son Quentin who was KIA in France during WWI. *Fred Bamberger*

Whether or not Lockheed's Robert Gross and other top-level management people knew that the British Purchasing Commission team was planning to visit the Burbank, Calif., factory in 1938, Kelly Johnson and Hall Hibbard rushed to get a Model 14 bomber design and mockup ready for the visit. The Commission generally liked with they saw, so a Lockheed team was invited to go to London for detailed negotiations. An original contract was for 200 airplanes by a specific delivery schedule. The British, believing that Lockheed would never even deliver 200 in the specified time, allowed that up to 50 additional plane deliveries would be acceptable within the time frame. All signatures required were on the contract by 23 June 1938. It is history that Lockheed delivered 250 airplanes on the original schedule. The Hudson Mk.V(LR) shown was the long-range version with extra fuel capacity. The British Air Ministry wanted what they called a General Reconnaissance aircraft, but they got far more than they bargained for. Those original B14 Hudsons were far superior to the cloth covered, low-powered Avro Ansons they would replace. The Hudson was produced in very large numbers for the RAF and the Commonwealth countries, as well as serving in many other services around the world. It proved to be a fine Lend-Lease airplane for all concerned. The Burbank production lines turned out no less than 2,941 Hudsons. . *NA via Gerry Markgraf*

BELOW & OVERLEAF   Six brand new Grumman TBF-1 Avengers were rushed to defend Midway Island (actually an atoll), as soon as Intelligence personnel had sufficient information about Imperial Japanese Navy intentions determined through code breakthroughs. Only one of the torpedo planes managed to return from battle and its damaged landing gear failed to operate correctly. The other five were distroyed. This photograph shows a new TBF-1, probably assigned to Torpedo 8 (VT-8), but the fuselage codes are not visible. However, it is known that the paint scheme of medium blue on upper surfaces and light grey on the lower portion seen here was also on the Midway Avengers. It has to be presumed that crew actions were at least partially posed for the photographer atop the flightline hangar at Bethpage, NY. As the pilot warms the 1600-hp Wright R-2600-8 engine, a second crewman climbs aboard while the third crewman receives some final instructions. At Midway, the failure of the first six Avengers deployed to inflict any damage at all in their attacks on the IJN targets is most likely to have been attributable to one or more of the following factors. They lacked fighter cover and there had been little or no training of crews on the new bombers. Tactics should have included coordinated dive bomber attacks to give the torpedo planes a chance of success. Of course USN torpedoes were all but worthless since there was certainly inability of the torpedoes to run true or

explode. Failure of the USN Ordnance Department to do intensive proof testing in peacetime years before December 7, 1941(in order to save money) was a pinchpenny decision that was not justifiable considering the war in Europe and Japanese actions in Asia.. The loss of several crews, inability to sink or damage critical targets, and the write-off of at least the five aircraft that never returned cannot be justified. Somebody made a bad decision at a command level but probably never even received a reprimand. "For want of a nail, a shoe was lost." Arguably, America had the worst torpedoes of any first-rate naval power. Just hold this thought in mind: What did the British Royal Navy Fleet Air Arm (FAA) have to attack the new, powerful Nazi battleship *Bismarck* with after she blew HMS *Hood* out of the water? "Stringbags!" The ancient (first flight in April 1934) Fairey Swordfish torpedo aircraft featured a fabric covered fuselage and biplane wings. A fixed landing gear was a major fixture, and power came from one 690 hp Bristol Pegasus radial engine. Every crew was given intensive instructions about attack modes in the 1930s. Fairey Swordfish were probably the second most successful torpedo planes of the war, demonstrating that at Taranto, Oran, and in the sinking of the modern battleship *Bismarck*. Subsequently, in roles other than as a torpedo aircraft, the Avengers performed admirably for years.   *Grumman/R. Starinchak*

Empennage and fuselage markings on this rare pairing of a North American SNJ-4 and a Curtiss SBC-4 were authorized only in post-Pearl Harbor months. As for the overall color of the aircraft, hues appear to be too dark for standard Non-specular Blue Grey, but if the paint was brand new it could be correct for a command aircraft. No sign of the underside color, Non-specular Light Grey, is evident unless the paint was not carried up the fuselage sides to any extent. The directive calling for this paint scheme for all carrier-based and ship-based aircraft was dated 13 October 1941. Furthermore, the markings on the SNJ-4 and SBC-4 appear to indicate the airplanes were assigned to the Commanding General, Fleet Marine Force, probably First Division, Wing 2 out of Quantico, Virginia. With the expansion moving rapidly, planes were frequently shifted around. The rudder striping and the red "meatball" centerpiece of the national insignia were cast aside officially in May 1942. On December 8, 1941 all hell broke loose at recruiting stations, active military and naval establishments, etc. Within hours or days at the most, factories producing any war equipment were shifted to seven-day-per-week schedules. It was as if there had been no warnings of impending war at all…and that flies in the face of reality. Hawaii's Territorial Newspaper, *The Honolulu Sunday Advertiser,* dated November 30, 1941, had these headlines: **KURUSU BLUNTLY WARNED NATION READY FOR BATTLE,** and this: **JAPANESE MAY STRIKE OVER WEEKEND!** That was not a cut-and-paste makeup story, although the current newspaper staff denies such headlines were published on that date. There is not the slightest clue to confirm their denial in this age of computers, none existing 60 years ago. That raises the critical question of why nearly everyone in Hawaii was partying or sleeping soundly on Saturday night. Additionally, evidence exists that a week after the attack on Pearl Harbor, USN personnel on ships at neutral ports in the Atlantic Ocean region were partying as if nothing had happened at all! Those reports were valid and true. The fact is that the Japanese were really not ready to strike, but command decisions based on IJA (Army) intelligence reports set the revised pace. Imagine the results if Japan had been ready to strike at the Aleutians and Alaska proper at the same time and follow up with invasion.
USMC / Author

ABOVE & BOTTOM OPPOSITE   Naval "specialists" seemed to have had some serious directional problems about camouflaging aircraft, especially right after we found ourselves at war with Japan, Germany, Italy and assorted minor nations. The movement away from the previously standardized grey tones to Blue Grey topside and Light Grey underside was mixed with the pre-war "meatball" national insignia and old Army Air Corps type tail stripes (13). All they were doing was making the airplanes more visible to any enemy. Not much time passed before the "meatball" disappeared, right along with the tail stripes....which had been eliminated from most AAC airplanes before the AAF was created. On training airplanes, such as these V-S OS2U-3 Kingfishers based at Pensacola or an at some Inshore Patrol Squadron base, there was no real reason to comply with earlier directives, and those seem to have caught up with reality. In fact, after the Battle of Coral Sea in May 1942, there was nearly universal agreement that far too much red paint was being applied to combat airplanes. With haste as the watchword, all red markings of any significance disappeared, replaced by simple, but larger, white stars on blue circles. All of the airplanes appear to be carrying yellow-painted practice bombs on the inboard shackles. (Although official data provided with these two images indicated the site was NAS Pensacola, visible clothing, terrain in the distance, and a building would strongly indicate such information was in error. There are many East Coast sites that could have had similar picture situations with Kingfishers.)   *USN/NA*

LEFT   If the American leadership did not have strong, realistic feelings that this country would be involved in a major war as the first year of the Forties decade opened, why was aircraft camouflage such a hotly disputed subject? Why did the Chief of the Air Corps, M/Gen. H. H. Arnold finally issue binding orders on 1 March 1939 to camouflage military aircraft? Even then B/Gen. George H. Brett, Chief of the Materiel Division, took exception to the paint and styles to be used. The intra-service arguments went on for years even prior to that time, but Arnold saw an immediate need. Although Curtiss P-40s, Bell P-39s, Consolidated B-24s and other aircraft for the Army Air Corps were coming off the production lines camouflaged, there were still serious arguments in progress about paint colors and styles of paint application. By 24 October 1940, they were still issuing directives about camouflage painting of aircraft, and the end was not in sight. As it was with many so-called first-line aircraft, this Curtiss P-40 (no suffix letter) was assigned to Luke Field, AZ, with many others as a school machine. By 22 October 1942, all "Plain Jane" P-40s in the AAF were placed in a Restricted category (no combat assignments) defined by an R prefix on the designator. Concurrently it is true that the RAF in North Africa was obtaining first-line service from the Tomahawk II version. The AVG (Flying Tiger Group) used most of the one hundred Tomahawk IIAs released by the RAF to China. Just to debunk one long-term illusion, the shark-tooth mouth markings did not originate with the AVG. They originated with the British forces in North Africa. *USAAF via G. Markgraf*

This Grumman F6F-3 is either the second or fourth production Hellcat to come off the Bethpage, NY, production line. The paint scheme appears to be quite correct per specifications, but time between painting and photographic time could have been a matter of months, accounting for the faded color compared to the paint on the Marine Corps SNJ-4 out of Quantico, Virginia. Grumman engineers made a complete break with all previous single-engine fighter configurations in designing the F6F series fighters. Serious studies led to the contract on 30 June 1941 for their G-50 design and two prototypes: an XF6F-1 powered by a Wright XR-2600-10 Cyclone 14; and an XF6F-2 model was planned, using an R-2600-16 engine to be fitted with a newly proposed Birmann turbosupercharger. The airframe was converted to utilize a Pratt & Whitney R-2800 engine, and designated XF6F-3. Flight testing of the XF6F-1 began one year after the contract was issued, and the XF6F-3 flew a month later. All a bit confusing, but BuAer and Grumman's team knew they needed all the guaranteed power they could get. The R-2800 Double Wasp was right for the job. On the USAAF side, when the XP-47B grew from the P-43A design, gross weight nearly doubled, but wing area only went up about 30 percent and power increased more than 50 percent. Grumman's situation did not stray far from those parameters in design of the XF6F-3, but it was, after all, also a carrier-based fighter. Testing of the first production F6F-3s took place at Bethpage July-August 1942, giving a good indication that the aircraft was producible as well as being a performer. It should be noted that wheel fairings on the early production example seen here were essentially unchanged from those used on prototypes. *Grumman*

Good Lord, this thing is as big and long as the Burlington *Zephyr* streamliner of the 1930s. But technically it is an XBLR-2 long-range bomber, fortunately redesignated XB-19 in war paint that must have added hundreds of pounds to its avoirdupois. Believe it or not, those men at work by the No. 3 engine are "propping" the engine. In other words, pulling it through to clear the cylinders. At least ten Douglas line workers are involved, and the tall ladder to the left was needed to slip the cuffs on the blade tips for this activity to take place. That outsized dome on top of the bomber is, really, a gun turret. It was supposed to enclose the gunner and his 37-mm American Armament Corp. cannon, but that "weapon" was really a fraud. (That company should have probably been indicted for that fraudulent offering.) This behemoth bomber, delivered in 1941, had a wingspan of no less than 212 feet and a length – not including that test boom or pseudo weapon – of no less than 132 feet 2 inches. That is 22 feet more than the wingspan of a Consolidated B-24 heavy bomber. Design gross weight was 160,332 pounds. Later in WWII, it acquired four Allison V-3420 liquid-cooled engines rated at 2600hp each to replace these Wright R-3350, 2000hp radial engines.   *Douglas Aircraft*

Although the Martin company's Baltimore owed a lot to the earlier XA-22 and foreign sales Model 167-F1 (British 167-B Maryland) as we might expect, it was mostly a new design, although originating with the dictates of the military specifications that led to the design of the AAC attack aircraft. If you have ever witnessed the landing of a Baltimore on a concrete runway, especially with an inexperienced pilot at the controls, you know that with the low-pressure tires it was a version of the Jersey Bounce. Compound that with the extra-large belly ferry tank and an emergency could turn into catastrophic results in seconds. The Royal Air Force desert camouflage paint scheme and long-range ferry tank on this Baltimore Mk.V are shown to perfection in this photograph. Final U.S. stop for most such Baltimores on their way to the Desert Air Force

in North Africa was Morrison Field, Florida. Final servicing for all types of aircraft flying the southern route across the Atlantic Ocean was accomplished at that large Air Transport Command base located immediately southwest of West Palm Beach. Even with 1,100 hp more than the Marylands they succeeded, Baltimores were no faster but did carry a larger bomb load. In April 1944, all production of Baltimore aircraft was halted after 1575 examples were produced, and orders for hundreds of additional improved versions were cancelled.   *G.L. Martin Company*

Lt. Fred Bamberger, then head honcho of the photographic section at Randolph Field – the "West Point of the Air", already famous in motion pictures based on training activities at that base – obviously had one of his photographers take his picture in color. Most likely, the camera used was his personal Contax, a wonderful 1930s 35mm German camera. The film had to be Kodachrome I, *the* only stable color film of the era. (The author's collection of such valuable material shows no sign of fading. Its "warm" color is unmatched by Ektachrome of Fujifilm color.) Fred was holding a 1930s 4x5 Graflex single-lens reflex press camera. Every exposure was accompanied by a loud 'caachunk' sound of the wind-up focal plane shutter. It was necessary to pull the slide from each cut film holder and then replace it before reversing the holder. Not as good, but faster, was the film pak. Thinner film was involved and you had to pull a tear-off paper tab to advance the film. As a press camera, the Graflex was hardly ideal for action shots. Shooting pictures of airplanes, race cars or trains in action meant "panning' the camera to match the vehicle's speed to avoid image distortion from focal plane shutter movement. Worse, you had to view the moving object through a telescoping affair above an angled mirror. Air-to-air picture taking could involve disorientation and the effects of a flapping bellows. Films were about one step from primitive daguerreotypes. Hauling this monster around all day could be less than fun. AAF pilot "Freddy" posed with Graflex on nothing less than a "Bamboo Bomber," technically a Cessna AT-17 Crane. *Fred Bamberger*

One of the rarest aircraft to be captured on Kodachrome in WWII days is the Vought SBU-1 or -2 biplane scout bomber from the mid 1930s, as a prototype. Strangely, the one captured by the photographer in this picture counts only as "wallpaper." The cameraman was far more interested in the 3-wheeler motorcycle, spectacular in its fire engine red paint and chrome-spoke wheels. This piece of Navy equipment was, per se, an extremely rare item. Suffice to say, the driver and his associate dressed in fire-resistant "Hot Papa" suits could not have been very comfortable in the sun. How many USN motorcycles could have fit that description? "Shooting" from a high angle and using a vertical format, the technician was forced to tilt his camera. Therefore, the SBU-1/-2 proved to be an inadvertent subject, however welcome. Vought Aircraft Division of United Aircraft Corp. had submitted the basic type to the USN as the XF3U-1 in a 2-seat fighter competition in 1932, but Grumman's first Navy fighter, the XFF-1 defeated all entrants and became the Navy's first standard fighter with retractable landing gear. Competition came from three fixed landing gear fighters – the Vought XF3U-1, Douglas XFD-1 and B/J XF2J-1 – and a nice looking parasol-wing Curtiss XF12C-1 with an even better looking retractable landing gear. The Curtiss proved to have one fault; it tended to come apart in the air. Vought let its fighter collect dust for two years, then submitted the virtually unchanged airplane as entrant in a new scout-bomber competition. Curtiss changed engines twice on the XF12C-1 loser after submitting it as a dive bomber competitor. It crashed once, was rebuilt only to crash to destruction. Ultimately it's BuNo. appeared on the fin of a totally new aircraft. It was a very different biplane, but evidently congressional investigators did not see through the deception. *USN via R. Starinchak*

LEFT When Vultee Aircraft, relocated in a new plant in Downey, California, produced a prototype BC-3 basic combat trainer in 1939, company executives expected to garner a production contract. However, that classification was abandoned by the Air Corps because North American AT-6As already served the same purpose. Major production contracts were awarded to that Inglewood company, evidently because it had an excellent airplane, well proven in time, very producible and priced right. Vultee's BC-3 was, perhaps, as good, but the die was cast. The company had another good product in their new BT-13 basic trainer, ousting NAA's BT-14 from the top position in that category. The result: large purchases of the Vultee were in order. As originally tested and ordered, streamlined fairings were installed on the rather simple landing gear struts as shown on a prototype marked with the Wright Field arrowhead emblem. After a short time, Vultee dispensed with the fairings at some change point where maintenance complications where encountered on airplanes not required to attain high speeds. *USAAF*

OPPOSITE TOP and BELOW   Although "Peace in our time" utterances from an unrealistic, appeasement-minded prime minister in England may have been convincing to wishful-thinking people in Europe in 1938, it seems to have had a different impact on America's military leaders. Perhaps it was the performance of the RAF's new Hurricanes and Spitfires. Performance of Germany's Messerschmitt Bf.109 fighters in the Spanish Civil War may have had an even greater influence. It seems that suddenly in late 1938 there was a realization among those leaders that the Air Corps' medium bombers were unlikely to survive against such existing fighters let alone even newer designs. Urgent specifications were issued in January 1939 for new medium bombers having speeds up to 350 mph while carrying two-ton bomb loads. America lacked any significant supply of trained multi-engine rated pilots, especially for new bombers having high wing loading, fast landing speeds and unheard of performance. It became abundantly clear to many high-ranking officials that new requirements for pilot qualifications called for high-performance twin-engine trainers. The military expansion program of 1940 was inspiration for Curtiss-Wright's Model CW-25, a side-by-side two-seat trainer bearing some resemblance in concept to Grumman's XF5F-1 Skyrocket Navy fighter. Because of alarm about an expected aluminum shortage, the prototype's fuselage featured a steel-tube structure with fabric skin. By the time Curtiss-Wright was awarded a production contract for an AT-9 trainer, the threatened shortage of aluminum failed to materialize; therefore a conventional aluminum monocoque fuselage structure was used in production. These "Jeep" trainers had more than adequate vertical tail surface and the engines were located as close as possible to the centerline of the aircraft in case of one-engine-out flight. Still, their accident ratios were high because they lacked feathering propellers. During the war, 791 of these AT-9 and AT-9A trainers were delivered to the AAF, but a high accident rate and availability of B-25s that were considered unacceptable for combat resulted in temporary and then permanent withdrawal from service at a fairly early date. These airborne Jeeps were sworn at and lauded by numerous pilot cadets. The closeup view reveals the P-39-like doors and the mid-thirties automotive "turret top" cabin.   *USAAF/Widewing*

Lost in the shuffle of trainers during the war was the Beech (Wichita plant) AT-10 pilot transition trainer, a contemporary of the Cessna AT-8 and Curtiss-Wright AT-9. Although the latter is well known in aviation circles, hardly anyone seemed to know that the AT-10 existed. Yet the Beech was built in far greater numbers: 1,771 were constructed at Wichita while Globe Aircraft manufactured 600 examples at the factory in Dallas, Texas. Fortunately, the improved technology for wooden aircraft construction had come along nicely at the right time (1939-41) to aid in conservation of strategic materials, mainly aluminum and steel. The only aluminum aircraft structure on the AT-10 was in the engine nacelles and cowling, plus the nose cap. All three of this group of advanced (transitional) trainers were powered by Lycoming R-680-9 aircooled radial engines rated at 295 hp each. Despite the divergence in design of all three training types, they were all rated at the same top speed. Of course speed differences existed between identical-appearing airplanes of the same model because of slight horsepower output, rigging and surface flaws. Beech built one version of the AT-10 with the Vee tail, later used on Beech's famed postwar Bonanza. *USAAF via Beech Aircraft*

Recalling Fox Movietone News films on theater screens of the 1940-41 era, an initial thought was about the contrast between British RAF pilots rushing to their Spitfire and Hurricane interceptor fighters during the Battle of Britain and these AAF fighter pilots about to fly their "400-mph" Curtiss P-40s! What is unclear is where did this casual event take place, and was it at a defensive fighter field or an advanced fighter-training base? Most modern fighting planes based in late 1941 on Oahu Island were Curtiss P-40Bs, some 87 of them lined up like ducks without ammunition or fuel at Wheeler Field for fear of saboteurs. There were also possibly thirty operational Curtiss P-36s on the field. Sabotage should have been the least of official worries. Warnings about Japanese attacks, at the very least, were everywhere a week before Dec. 7, 1941. This photograph may well have been taken weeks before December 1941 at Wheeler Field. Or it could have been a typical scene at any major air base operated by the new USAAF. It is not likely, at this late date, that we will ever know for certain. *AAF via Robert D. Archer*

BELOW and OPPOSITE   In the immediate period following the Pearl Harbor attack, many hundreds of Lend-Lease airplanes procured from Curtiss by the British Commonwealth with U.S. funding were repossessed as emergency measures against other unknown Japanese moves. Derived from the small number of P-40Ds built, the British Purchasing Mission bought 560 as Kittyhawk Mk I models. A significant change was introduced forward of the windshield – which also changed – with the installation of an Allison F-series engine featuring external-spur reduction gearing. This shortened the nose and raised the thrust line. Military power was raised to 1150 hp with greater reliability. Purchased under the Lend-Lease Program, 1500 Kittyhawk Mk IAs were to be supplied to Great Britain, the AAF designation being P-40E-1-CU. Firepower was increased to six .50-caliber machine guns, all wing mounted. It should be noted that many Kittyhawk IAs were repossessed by the USAAF when war engulfed this country, many went to Commonwealth Countries, and there were losses during transport by sea. This P-40E-1-CU, cloaked in RAF camouflage but flown by and for the USAAF was filmed at Hensley Field, Texas, otherwise known as NAS Dallas. It carries a belly drop tank and the star and meatball insignia of the AAF. Kittyhawks were not used at any time in the defense of the British Isles. On the subject of P-40Ds and Es and Kittyhawks, there is no doubt that Curtiss produced one

massive number of fighters. But they were all essentially derivatives of the basic Hawk 75 designed by Donovan Berlin as project engineer in 1934 after he left Northrop. The Curtiss Airplane Division fell flat on its face when given the assignment to build Republic P-47Gs. Not one was ever capable of commitment to combat. When somebody produced buggy whips long after they became unwanted, what good was that? Curtiss was producing a 1934 wing and tail and fuselage and landing gear in 1944! Their useless new designs like the XP-60 series travesties and the XP-62 caricature were useless wastes of time and effort. At the same time, with Walter Tydon in Berlin's chair, corporate nonsense ignored his XP-40Q possibilities. As shown by the ultimate performance of the XP-40Q-2, they could have been a close contemporary of the P-51D in production at about the same time. But corporate management would have made certain the type was never as good as any P-51. Poor Walt Tydon never had his chance at fame. Curtiss could produce 'Non-state-of-the-art' P-40s as long as the customer tolerated them. Supermarine *never* suffered from that disease that afflicted C-W throughout WWII. Cookie-cutter P-40D/E production lines are shown awaiting workers in wartime. *Fred Bamberger(1), Curtiss(1)*

LEFT ABOVE & BELOW Vengeance was the name of Vultee Aircraft's V-72 dive bomber, but against whom? Vultee's propensity for designing cookie-cutter airplanes where subassemblies could be interchanged with alacrity to change operational functions only really worked on training aircraft. The British Purchasing Mission team must have been far more desperate for aircraft than anyone could believe to purchase such monstrosities as the Vengeance while rejecting Lockheed 322-B Lightnings. "What looks good must be good," certainly was forgotten in this design. Obviously no Vultee engineer ever was allowed to use a French curve or a ship's curve. The vertical tail was an isosceles triangle with the top part amputated, calculated and drawn in minutes, and the only reason the cowling was round was because the engine was that shape. Britain ordered so many that Vultee had to establish a new production line at the factory in Nashville, Tenn., while Northrop's new factory at Hawthorne, Calif. had space to spare for another line. Army Air Corps orders were placed in 1941, but only to expedite deliveries authorized by President Roosevelt's signing of the Lend-Lease Bill. As a consequence, the A-31 designation was assigned so the AAF could order 100 from Vultee and 200 from Northrop. Nobody had figured out that no dive bomber was going to be protected by a rear gunner facing backward; why not make it a lighter, smaller and faster single-seater to do the job? Vultee's A-35A version for the USAAF met all Army specifications while A-35B had an extra 100 hp from the R-2600-13 Cyclone 14. AAF models did little more than tow gunnery targets for the duration. At least one outspoken AAF general was quoted as saying that A-31/A-35 Vengeances were "a shining example of the waste of material, manpower and time in the production of an airplane" which his Directorate of Military Requirements office had "tried to eliminate for several months." Evidently Knudsen's War Production Board was not even listening (one more time). The British used their Vengeance dive bombers in Burma, replacing older, slower twin-engine Blenheims. With adequate fighter cover, they performed well in that jungle environment. An official reason for keeping the V-72/A-31/A-35 in production centered on "keeping the workforce intact until they could switch to Lockheed P-38 production." The factory finally turned out 114 Lightnings! That changeover should have occurred 18 critical months earlier. *Northrop via Robt. Archer (2)*

ABOVE and PAGES 152 and 153   Despite many warning signs pertaining to Japanese intentions in the Western Pacific frontier, the United States Army and Navy seemed to have botched the matter of espionage as if they were rank amateurs in such matters. Britain's performance in that field was no better, perhaps not even as good since communications between Singapore and London over a lengthy period were viewed with disdain. Evidently the designers of fortifications at that British naval base never even considered the possibilities of massive air attacks or overland invasion routes. Therefore the defenses against a Japanese Army invasion were underarmed and undermanned. Contrary to U.S. Navy's love affair with dive-bombing, little interest developed in the Fleet Air Arm of the Royal Navy or the RAF for half a decade. They seemed indifferent to the tactics until the Air Ministry ordered two prototypes of the Blackburn Skua in April 1935. These also proved to be the forerunners of the first operational monoplanes and dive-bombers in the FAA. They served in three squadrons and were in combat until mid-1941 when they were replaced by airplanes not suited to dive-bombing targets. Vultee Vengeance dive-bombing aircraft were not even considered until the successes scored by *Luftwaffe* Junkers Ju 87 Stukas were observed. Contracts for Vengeance aircraft were placed with Vultee in mid summer 1940 following the collapse of France, orders being based entirely on a design plus performance projections. Orders were for a total of 700 Mk.I and Mk.2 were placed. Unlike Lockheed (Hudson) and North American (Apache/Mustang) performances in expedited delivery, a year passed before the first Vengeance flew (July 1941). Another twelve months elapsed before the first production airplane took off. By that time the entire dive-bombing concept had been forced to change. The 2-seat dive-bomber was history against well-defended targets by 1943 when Lockheed P-38s proved in the MTO that they were more efficient at bombing land and sea targets, and they then were able to provide their own defense. During the invasion of *Festung Europa,* Republic P-47Ds and Hawker Typhoons set the standards for the tactic against land targets. Douglas A-24s, Curtiss A-25s and the Vengeance A-31/A-35 types became targets of opportunity for the enemy. Indeed, A-31s and A-35s did become targets by towing sleeve targets for training of gunners in subsequent months.   *Northrop via Gerald Balzer (3)*

Few people born after 1945 would recognize the reflecting pool in Washington, D.C., as it was in the busy days of World War II, especially as viewed from the heights of Washington's Monument. Acres of temporary buildings served to accommodate thousands of Navy Department employees. Even in the early 1930s when governmental stress was on solving the nation's faltering economy and the National Recovery Act (NRA) was being touted as the solution to all of our financial and well-being problems, central Washington was lacking in signs of hustle and bustle. That scene changed radically during WWII. Memories: I spent part of the summer in 1933 at the home of my uncle, Capt. Harry Tunis (AAC Ret.), in what seemed to be a country town far from the nation's capital. That town was Silver Spring, now well within the encircling I-95/I-495 interstate highway system. (Capt. Harry Tunis was the victim of an old flight maneuver called the Cross-over. His lead Boeing P-12 was suddenly crunched from above by another P-12 in the formation. Somehow, Harry was able to bail out, but his back was broken. Author)   *A. U. Schmidt*

Having taken on a topcoat of camouflage paint in accordance with Materiel Command edict, one of the more interesting B-17 Flying Fortresses in the AAF early in 1942 was this Boeing B-17C. It became a movie star of sorts in 1942 when she played a major part in the film, *Air Force* featuring then current star, John Garfield. In that film, the airplane bore the name "Mary Ann." She spent a large amount of time heading west to encounter Japanese forces in the Philippines and other places in Southeast Asia. In the film, it became an early B-17 with a tail gun, thanks to Garfield and a hacksaw to remove the plastic tail cone. Once clear, it was supposedly a cinch to install a .50-cal. machine gun. No, it wasn't a "surplus" airplane because the War Assets Administration had not even been created at the time. It was a real AAF bomber-trainer. For recruiting and publicity purposes they changed the name to "Mary Ann, Star of Air Force" after the film was released.   *USAAF   (2)*

LEFT and OPPOSITE Looking Backward. It is almost a revelation to read some of the best pre-Pearl Harbor writing about America and where it stood in the first months of 1941. *Fortune* magazine for March was published by Time, Inc., in their large – 11x14 inches – format as an expensive ($2.00) issue with no less than 240 pages! It was all about U.S. Air Power. A major editorial about that power was authored by famed military and naval correspondent for the New York *Times,* Hanson W. Baldwin. His article ridiculed isolationist Sen. Burton Wheeler for his January announcement that "the U.S. armed services did not possess a single plane fit for battle conditions in Europe." Baldwin called that an absurdity. Wheeler was a gadfly, but he was to be proven correct within a year. Strangely, Baldwin went on to verify Wheeler's contention, but he pointed out that our best materiel was going to Britain. As a result he admitted that we were barely a second-rate air power. But his argument was that it was America's great industrial capacity to produce aircraft that was of far greater importance. Unfortunately, Mr. Baldwin, an Annapolis graduate, based his premise "on the grand concept of sea power as the first line of defense." The U.S. aircraft industry did $225 million worth of business in 1939. By 1941, that was projected to rise to $3 billion in military orders alone. However, Consolidated Aircraft's huge Fort Worth factory was still a plan, and Ford Motor Co. did not even have a plan for a massive Willow Run Bomber Plant! Britain had started their "Shadow Factory" scheme well before war erupted in Europe, and it probably saved that nation via the Battle of Britain. America was yet to show its trump card. In the meantime, three images taken sometime during 1941 in Grumman Aircraft's Bethpage, N.Y. plant would hardly begin to support the "50,000 planes a year" dream of President Roosevelt. Two women working alone on early F6F naval fighters cannot be encouraging, while only a handful of workers are seen in a jam-packed TBF-1 Avenger fuselage and wing clutter. Far less encouraging is the view of what purports to be a Final Assembly bay with Wildcat fighters, British Goose amphibian and assorted powerplant assemblies crammed so tightly together that walking space was at a premium. Out in California, Douglas' Santa Monica main assembly hangar was not much better, but work could continue outdoors winter and summer. A new assembly building had just been completed for new C-54 transport production late in 1941, and a huge modern factory had been erected at Long Beach Airport. Perhaps fastest growing of all was Lockheed Aircraft out in the San Fernando Valley. Starting with the Lockheed Hudson contract for the British in 1938, assembly and component plants grew at a fabulous rate. The Sleeping Giant was finally awake. And as history shows, none too soon. The special issue of *Fortune* was dated March 1941. On 20 June, the new United States Army Air Forces was created with General H. H. Arnold as the new Chief, Army Air Forces. (That was the correct nomenclature.) *Northrop-Grumman History Unit (3)*

ABOVE   Women served in fairly large numbers in the U.S. Army as WAFs (Women's Army Forces), Marine Corps and USN (WAVES) in World War II, but none served their country better than the essentially non-military (I wonder why) WASPs. It was often a dangerous job, and all know that more flyers were killed in testing and training than in combat. Being a ferry pilot was not without its dangers. Although not officially sworn into the military and naval services, WASPs flew virtually every type of airplane from observation and liaison types to twin-engine fighters, multi-engine bombers and transports. No fewer than 1,074 females served in the Women Airforce Service Pilots organization, essentially in a status about equal to men in the Merchant Marine. WASPs Barbara Erickson-London (at left) and Evelyn Sharp (dressed in a casual WAF uniform with civilian blouse) chit-chatted with a USAAF pilot at North American Aviation's Inglewood, Calif., plant in 1942. Erickson-London is turned out in nearly universal civilian work clothing with a standard seat pack parachute ready to depart in that A-36 attack aircraft or one nearby. This view is looking north from the NAA parking area toward the Mines Field runways and the airline and manufacturing buildings on the north side. All aircraft normally departed westerly toward the ocean, passing over Sepulveda Blvd. before reaching the nearby coastline. The Douglas El Segundo Plant hangars and aircraft parking area were to the left of this group of pilots. Masking tape on the A-36's wings was temporary coverage over the machine gun ports. *USAAF via author*

OPPOSITE Huge grocery stores, even in most big cities like Detroit, Los Angeles or Chicago as the decade of the 1930s ended, were a rarity. Out in Southern California's big cities (or even towns like San Diego or Sacramento) it was far more commonplace – in a nation of about 120 million total population– to encounter open-front markets where all fresh produce was right out in front in the open, in many cases all night. No crowds populated the aisles, especially in the later evening hours. Prices were especially attractive, particularly for navel oranges in California. Once outside of New York and Pennsylvania, the areas known as Middle America and the South, things were often radically different. Even A&P and Kroger grocery stores, considered the big chains, on main streets of neighborhoods were generally only a double store-front size. In small towns or the suburbs, pickle barrels might be encountered in the stores. Viewed in an unknown part of Kansas City in Kansas (and Missouri) in 1942 where the great Missouri River divided the city, this tiny grocery might well have been a hangover from the first decade of the century or it most certainly had survived the Depression. Without newspaper inserts, the only real way to advertise "Specials" or great prices was to plaster the glass front with signs. If you envy the prices, just know that in 1941 an experienced aircraft worker was probably lucky to be earning 90 cents an hour for a 48-hour week. In the Midwest, if premium pay was in effect for that employee, his gross pay might have been around $50.00 a week for a 6-day schedule.[6]
R. Starinchak

[6]The author was graduated after attending a technical high school (aviation) in Detroit, Mich., in June 1941 with a scholarship to G.M. Tech. Immediately upon reaching age 18 on July 11, 1941, I was hired the same day by Ex-Cell-O Tool & Die. Income went to $65.00 per week average, (with overtime) by October, incredible pay for factory workers below toolmaker status following the Depression.

159

LEFT & BELOW   Fortunately for America, when President Franklin D. Roosevelt addressed Congress on May 16, 1939, to request legislation to support production of 50,000 airplanes a year, everyone involved realized that pilots to fly such numbers of aircraft had to be trained in greatly expanded programs. Suddenly, pilot training became a top priority. The military and naval service quickly realized that such programs reached far beyond anything they or their facilities could handle. In that same month, the Air Corps started awarding contracts to nine established flight training schools across America. One of the first schools to win such a contract was the Ryan Aeronautical Corp. school located adjacent to Consolidated Aircraft's relatively new plant in San Diego at Lindbergh Field. On the west side of the airport, a civilian installation, Ryan's factory was manufacturing aircraft on a relatively small scale. Their Model ST, STA and ST-M Menasco-powered two-seat trainers were popular in USA and overseas. The primary training schools around the country routinely used Stearman PT-13 and PT-17 biplanes (Navy models N2S and NAF N3Ns), but the Ryan school had their own products, low-wing PT-16, PT-20, PT-21 and PT-22 derivative of the basic type. Soon, Menasco 125 hp engines became unobtainable, and the most popular substitution was Kinner radial engine. Within a short time, Ryan produced 1,048 Kinner-powered PT-22 and PT-22A. One of the PT-22 series trainers is shown during a training session where the young cadets were instructed on the characteristics and operation of the trainer type they were about to fly. Another PT-22, equipped with the Kinner R-540-1 aircooled radial engine is shown in flight. Training planes were rarely camouflaged, generally remaining marked with typical Air Corps pre-war markings. The metal-fuselage Ryan trainers never proved to be as popular as Fairchild's PT-19 trainers using Ranger engines. Maintenance on the Ryans was much more difficult for several reasons, even according to Ryan school personnel. *NA via R. Starinchak*

LEFT Luke Field, Arizona, was a pretty logical place for all-year flight training in the late 1930s and early '40s because of weather conditions. It got an assignment for advanced training of pilots who made it successfully through basic training, largely at Randolph Field, Texas. Some of the advanced trainers at times included Boeing P-12 biplanes, but that was all right because the Navy was still using Grumman F3F fighters for that same purpose. Some of the equipment included this North American AT-6C-NT (AC41-32161) that was built in Dallas, Texas, and a Curtiss RP-40B. One amazing thing about the Texan trainer was the rather ludicrous fact that the national insignia on the fuselage appears to be painted upside down. The white star was completely disoriented, and evidently nobody had even noticed. It must have left the factory in that non-conforming position. Lord knows in what pattern the wing insignias had been applied. *USAAF via Robt. Archer*

RIGHT While the initial combat events were taking place in Hawaii at Pearl Harbor, T.H., Lockheed in Burbank was manufacturing a continuous line of Lockheed 322-B Lightnings under terms of the British contract. When the Air Ministry in England chose to cancel the contract without proof that the airplanes failed to meet design and contract specifications, they were obviously on course for a court confrontation. Wouldn't that have been a fine kettle of fish for the politicians to deal with. The Pearl Harbor attack by the Japanese had one good result, at least. The U.S. Government took over all undelivered 322-Bs under the war emergency powers situation. Many RAF Lightnings were stored outdoors in a field hard by Hollywood Way in Burbank. We know that 22 of the 322-Bs remained virtually unchanged when they went to the Fourth Training Command as P-322-Is or otherwise did not become trainers for the AAF. Evidently Lockheed re-engined another 121 of the Lightnings with Allison V-1710F-2 engines, using P-38D or E cowling components. No turbosuperchargers were ever installed in 322-B airplanes and the re-engined 322-Bs became P-322-II's The Lightning seen during some engine runup exercise with a civilian in the cockpit and two civilian workers in the background with the ground support equipment must have been at some depot base. It was not Burbank. *AAF via R. Starinchak*

Flexible gunnery had its place in aviation from the earliest days of World War I, and things were not radically changed for certain aircraft in the first few years of WWII. Here we have an experienced weapons instructor in the aft seat of one of those middle '30s Curtiss SBC-3 or perhaps -4 scout dive bombers that were still serving aboard the USN's major aircraft carriers even well after war had erupted between major powers in Continental Europe. What should have set off alarm bells throughout naval headquarters was the clear fact that a PB2Y Coronado flying boat was faster than any SBC. Add a 500-lb. bomb under the SBC, and speed was about 200 mph. Typical naval scout bombers were armed with one forward firing .30-cal. machine gun and one flexible weapon of equal caliber in the aft gunner's position. Fortunately for all concerned, SBCs never dropped any bombs in anger. Even the superceding Vought SB2U-2s and -3s fared badly in the few combat engagements to which they had been committed, such as the Battle of Midway Island. Although they matched the current IJN dive bombers and torpedo bombers in performance in 1942, they had to face the Mitsubishi Zero fighters assigned to defense of IJN aircraft carriers and their bombing aircraft. Two squadrons of Vought SBU-1 biplanes served as the main scouting and bombing aircraft aboard the USS *Hornet* well into 1941 in VS-41 and VS-42. Apparently a protracted takeoff run kept the succeeding Vought SB2U Vindicator type from operating safely from *Hornet*. A serious number of rear gunners aboard aircraft like the Douglas TBD-1, Douglas SBDs, Vought SB2Us, Grumman TBF-1s and similar combat aircraft lost their lives in combat while providing minimal protection for the aircraft in which they flew. *NA via R. Starinchak*

An interesting view of an unusual early Lockheed P-38F from a lofty perspective reveals that this fighter version of the Lightning is fully armed; yet it has been coated with haze blue paint that was previously only applied to the early F-4 reconnaissance versions. It can only be assumed that experimental trials were being made for the photographic airplanes, perhaps using a fighter because new production aircraft were undergoing transformation to the Army Reconnaissance (then F category) configuration alongside the Lockheed airstrip at Plant B. Camouflage specialists have been unable to provide any other explanation. From the exhaust stains and fading of the flat blue paint on the P-38F, it is obvious that some serious operational hours have been logged. It could have been a service test airplane from Patterson Field, Ohio, or from Eglin Field, Florida. Many minor mysteries accrued during America's involvement in World War II. Of great importance, however, is the fact that P-38Fs performed a feat in 1942 that no other mass-produced fighter aircraft in the world could have accomplished with any degree of success. Since no Allied fighter of any type could then escort 8th Air Force B-17Es or other bombers much beyond the French coast, long-ranging P-38 fighters were desperately needed. German submarine activity was responsible for sinking great numbers of ships between America and England. Loss of even one ship could mean the loss of many fighters. Operation BOLERO was created around the Lockheed P-38F, when nearly 200 of the Lightnings were flown over a pioneering route by their assigned fighter pilots to assigned bases in England with minimal losses not at all attributable to aircraft or engine failures. The "Arsenal" had become a traveling road show.   *USAAF/Robert D. Archer*

When one considers that the Republic P-47 Thunderbolt, a direct outgrowth of the Seversky AP-4 was predestined to become one of the greatest fighter aircraft of WWII, it defies logic that in the crucial days of 1940 the Materiel Division only ordered one prototype of the XP-47B. Single prototype losses were associated with the Boeing 299-X (XB-17), Lockheed XP-38, Grumman XP-50, North American NA-40B, and the XP-47B was nearly abandoned on its first flight when smoke filled the cockpit. Fortunately, test pilot Lowery Brabham made the decision to stay with the airplane until he analyzed the situation fully. He managed a safe landing. Actually, the XP-47B was a very evolutionary design. Seversky's AP-4 did catch fire and crashed, but it was the absolute pioneer of aft-mounted turbosuperchargers in a fighter aircraft. The Air Corps, recognizing the performance demonstrated, ordered an advanced version in service test quantity as the YP-43. By that time, Seversky had become Republic Aviation. In order to keep the plant operational, several orders came along for production P-43 Lancers. With the growing need for a fast interceptor, Republic built a mockup of their AP-4J design with a new XR-2800 engine. Already halfway to what became the eventual goal, General Echols' Materiel Division at Wright Field worked out a new set of specifications after discussions with the top officers of the combat arm of the Air Corps at that time, namely the GHQ Air Force. During a short meeting at Dayton, Ohio, Mr. Kartveli and his associates were directed to stop work on the XP-44, cancel all effort on the XP-47/XP-47A and move on to build a new XP-47B. The successful prototype – still not the ultimate design – was the precursor of 15,682 additional Thunderbolts. They were flown in combat by America, Great Britain, France, China, Mexico, Russia and Argentina during the war years with almost universally good success.   *Rudy Arnold*

Wars are not fought entirely in the daylight hours, although the U.S. Army Air Corps seemed to believe that was the case even as Great Britain deployed Bristol Beaufighter IF series night fighters against Nazi bombers that had switched to raids in darkness in an attempt to avoid excessive losses. Two RAF squadrons became fully operational with Beaufighters on 17 September 1940 using A.I.Mk.IV radar equipment. The British also converted some Douglas Bostons to night fighter configurations, the conversion being identified by the name Havoc. Early in 1941, M.I.T. established a radiation laboratory to develop airborne interception radars (A.I.). The first contract to Douglas for A-20-DEs was for a high-altitude bomber with turbosupercharged Wright R-2600 engines. When that engine version proved to be unavailable for production, sixty of the 63 airplanes on order were completed as P-70 night fighters carrying four 20-mm cannons in a belly pannier. One of these was the development XP-70. Assigned to combat Japanese bombers in the Pacific war zones, the P-70s were found to be ineffective against bombers flying at 25,000 feet. Some early series P-38s in zone were converted with the same radar sets as an interim measure pending arrival of Northrop P-61 Black Widows. *USAAF via R. Starinchak*

165

Flying boat and amphibian builder Sikorsky, part of United Aircraft Corporation in the late 1930s, manufactured S-43 amphibians having the wingspan of a Lockheed P-38 and physical characteristics of a Consolidated Model 28 or PBY-5A. The most significant difference was in the fuselage with a passenger compartment type fuselage compared to the patrol bomber hull of the Catalina series. Both types had two wing-mounted engines, pylon-mounted, strut-braced wings, landing gear retracting into the hull sides and a single vertical tailplane. Sikorsky supplied the USN with no less than seventeen of these amphibians as JRS-1s for use by Navy and Marine utility squadrons, seating as many as nineteen aboard. So precarious was America's patrol airplane situation immediately after the Pearl Harbor assault that at least one JRS-1 was equipped with underwing depth charges mounted on racks outboard of the nacelles to combat the submarine menace. It was based at NAS Ford Island in the days following the destructive attack on our capital ships of the Pacific Fleet. Markings on the camouflage-painted airplane included 13 alternating red and white tail stripes and the pre-war star-and-meatball national insignia. Some confusing data have been published about other Sikorsky flying boat transports: One Sikorsky S-42 former PAA 4-engine flying boat flew with Naval Transport Sqdn. VR-2 with the most unusual squadron marking 1-R-2-S. It was obviously a former PAA trans-Atlantic airliner, misidentified as the JR2S-2 (BuNo. 12390). Three JR2S-1 airplanes were actually the three Sikorsky VS-44A transports belonging to American Export Airlines and operated under Navy contract for the duration of the war. USN BuNos. 12390 through 12392 were assigned to those very large 4-engine VS-44A flying boats. It is far more likely that the S-42 did not carry a naval designator unless someone unfamiliar with the aircraft inexplicably assigned the JR2S-2 designator. Evidence exists that the S-42 was moored off Banana River, Florida, on 4 June 1942. The two surviving Martin M-130 Clippers, including the ultra-famous "China Clipper," were also operated by Pan American Airways under contract with BuNos. 48230 and 48231 applied. However, no formal USN designators were ever assigned. Confusion was rampant as 1942 dawned.   *USN via James Sullivan*

Lockheed Hudsons as originally ordered by the British Purchasing Commission stemmed from an April 1938 unscheduled visit of that body to Lockheed's factory located at the intersection of Empire Ave. and Victory Place in Burbank, California. The visitors inspected a hastily created Type B14 mockup based on the civil Model 14 Super Electra, the same basic type (a Model 14-N2) in which oilman Howard Hughes circled the globe in record time from July 10 to 14, 1938. Just about three weeks earlier, the BPC signed a contract worth an outstanding $25 million, covering the cost of 200 Model B14Ls coastal reconnaissance bombers. As an added incentive for expedited delivery of these much needed aircraft, the BPC would buy as many more B14Ls as could be delivered by December 1939, capped at 250 aircraft. The British referred to the new type as the Hudson. A power turret, something hardly known in the USA, manufactured by Boulton Paul and fitted with two .303-in. machine guns was to be installed in the aft fuselage of each Hudson, primarily upon delivery of the airplanes to the UK. Considered impossible from an upstart company, at least by other key manufacturers in America, Lockheed's Plant B delivered 250 Hudsons nearly two months ahead of the deadline. It must be noted that between 10 December 1938 – the first flight date of a production Hudson – and May 1943, no less than 2,941 Hudsons in various models were delivered to various services of the Allies. Deliveries included 217 of the AT-18 gunnery trainers (as shown) fitted with a more modern power turret produced by Martin. It was also fitted with twin .50-cal. machine guns.   *Lockheed*

One American export warplane that came along at just the right time to provide much needed assistance to the French and British was Consolidated Aircraft's Model 32 bomber, later designated as the Liberator. The airplane, derived from the company's private venture Model 31 commercial flying boat developed to exploit the high-aspect-ratio Davis wing design, was essentially a four-engine, high-wing bomber having numerous characteristics of the flying boat. Design work on the Model 32 was not even initiated until 1939. In January of that year, chief engineer I. M. Laddon and other company engineers were invited to Wright Field to confer with Air Corps chief, M/Gen. H. H. Arnold and B/Gen. Oliver Echols regarding a need for another four-engine long-range bomber as stable mate to the Boeing B-17E model then in development. A speed of at least 300

mph, a 35,000 ft. service ceiling and a range of 3,000 miles were requirements. Construction of a mockup began before the month ended. A contract for just one prototype XB-24 and the mockup was signed by 30 March. It is interesting to note that the Model 31 civil flying boat had not even been launched when the Model 32 (XB-24) contract was signed. That flying boat finally slipped into San Diego Bay in May 1939, having proceeded down the launching ramp on its own retractable tricycle beaching gear. The pug-nosed XB-24 prototype made its first flight on 29 December 1939 with test pilot Bill Wheatley at the controls, just nine days after Consolidated received a then mammoth 200 plane Navy contract for production of PBY-5 Catalina flying boats. Huge plant expansions in San Diego involved tremendous hiring programs. As one example, the aircraft company employment stood at less than 3,000 on 1 January 1940, up from a lean 1,200 a year earlier. By October 1941 the payroll stood at 24,000! Another example of the trends in the Arsenal of Democracy at that time is cited: The first *production* contract for seven service test YB-24s was placed three days before the experimental XB-2and mockup were ordered. And that was only the beginning. Three of 2,425 San Diego-built B-24Ds are shown with trainer markings in loose formation. *AAF via G. Markgraf (2)*

In World War I days, when the air combat action was most likely taking place at less than 100 mph, a rear gunner was really necessary to protect light bomber and observation airplanes from fighters with a twenty percent speed advantage. By the mid 1930s, with speeds having doubled and rear gunners still using .30-cal. machine guns without great hitting power and still in the "ring and bead" age of sighting, the "backseat gunner" – like the one in this Vought-Sikorsky OS2U – was superfluous. As General Ben Kelsey was inclined to say, "The gunner is facing backward, trying to track a target. The pilot, facing forward, knows immediately when he will maneuver, so when he 'zigs' for evasion the gunner is 'zagging' and he never catches up." American fighter pilots in WWII had to have proof positive, for the most part, to have a confirmed "kill" chalked up for them. Bomber gunners had no positive camera record, and with several bombers in "box formation" blasting away at every moving fighter, who could ever be positive about which gunner brought down an enemy aircraft? No supportable records exist to prove that any given AAF, USN or USMC gunner can positively claim credit for knocking down an enemy attacker. But maybe it gave the pilot a sense of "somebody watching his back." Worse, decades of movies have shown backseat gunners "killing" enemy aircraft in droves, giving a false impression of real life.   *NA/R. Starinchak*

One amazing fact about the old Army Air Corps (AAC) and the brand new Army Air Forces that came into being on 20 June 1941 was the near total lack of fast reconnaissance airplanes. In fact there is every probability that Lt. Col. George Goddard was still in possession of a few of the ancient (1920s) Fairchild F-1 aerial survey airplanes, although even those had been redesignated C-8 (transports). However, the light finally dawned, perhaps after they read about the DeHavilland Mosquito recon airplanes in the European War. The AAC ordered fourteen modified commercial Model B18s (not the Douglas bomber) purchased as F-2s for aerial mapping. After modifying C-45 airplanes for mapping, they ordered no fewer than 42 of the type as F-2Bs. But they were not really suitable for use in aerial reconnaissance work. (Two F-2Bs from Wright Field are seen in the photograph.) Later, the AAF ordered one Douglas A-20 converted to become an F-3 camera-carrying airplane with T-3A camera equipment in the bomb bay. Finally (then) Col. George Goddard was heard. Two Lockheed P-38Es were ordered as F-4-1-LOs by a Change Order, becoming America's first high-speed recon aircraft. Soon the AAF was on its way to having 97 additional F-4s. Initial deliveries were in March 1942. It must have been only days before F-4s were on the scene for OPERATION TORCH in North Africa. Hundreds more of varied photo-reconnaissance versions followed. The Lightnings became the best aircraft for that duty in the AAF during the war. Only the Mosquito, F-6 Mustang and PR Spitfires were in the same league. It seems beyond belief that America should have been so remiss about developing recon aircraft until war was inevitable. Every general now knows that no army or navy can survive and win without substantial aerial reconnaissance. It is the very heart of survival. If any one man can be given credit for the turnaround, it was Goddard. But even his genius could not make the P-51D the equal of an F-5. Nothing the AAF had in service in WWII could match the F-5F and especially the F-5F-3-LO (converted P-38L-5-LOs) for range and overall performance. Comparing the P-51D to P-38s is like comparing a 1999 Grand Prix Formula 1 racer to an Indianapolis type racer of a previous year. It is ludicrous. The Allison powered Mustang was on its way out when it had the good fortune to be wedded to the Merlin engine. The far older basic P-38 design (think P-38 to P-51) mated to Merlins or especially Griffons, which it could easily handle, would have been the king. No way was GM's Bill Knudsen going to end Allison engine production in favor of Packard and Rolls-Royce. Elephants would fly first.   *Fred Bamberger*

This crewman is fortunate in having an "inside job' in an aging YB-17, a relatively old Boeing "Flying Fortress" in need of a "bouncer," so this waist gunner was equipped with a .50-cal. machine gun. Boeing Y1B-17s – later designated YB-17s – although tiny in numbers, served on in the AAF as gunnery training planes for familiarization after being declared unfit for combat. This one was based at Langley Field, Virginia. Only thirteen Y1B-17s were delivered to the AAC in 1937 to function as Service Test examples, frequently operating out of Wright Field or Patterson Field, Ohio. *Widewing Archive*

Beam gunners on Consolidated PBY-1 through –3 models were only protected from the elements by sliding covers, meaning they were unprotected from wind, rain, snow and all other weather – even in the Aleutians or over the North Atlantic Ocean while firing the single machine gun on each side. On subsqusequent PBY-4 and -5 versions bulbous Plexiglas teardrop turrets (unpowered) at the beam positions were each equipped with one .50-cal. Browning machine gun; the other three weapons were all .30-caliber Brownings. The gunner had reasonably good armor protection and an enviable clear field of fire. Ordnance carried by the PBY Catalinas consisted of up to 1,000 lbs of bombs or depth charges. Something not generally known is that NAS Ford Island (later, NAS Pearl Harbor) was the primary naval air station for Oahu in 1941. It was quite a small station. What was later to become NAS Honolulu was an expansion of the local civil airport, an Army Corps of Engineers project. Work was only about five percent complete on December 7, 1941. The main military airports at the time were the Army's Hickham Field and Wheeler Field. *USN/NA*

171

John K. Northrop was evidently a Thomas A. Edison of aviation. Even without the formal documents to prove he was an engineer compared, for instance, to Grover Loening, he had the genius to design the original Lockheed Vega in wood. Almost immediately after that, he designed the all-metal Northrop Alpha I, having made a giant stride forward in stressed-skin monoplane design, again with full-monocoque fuselage structures. (Rather strangely, Northrop's brief biography did not appear in the prestigious "The Bluebook of Aviation" in 1932. He probably did not submit his resume.) Then, of course, he went on to real fame in design and development of the profoundly futuristic flying wing series of aircraft that will be forever connected with his name. This rare photograph of JKN together with the remarkably advanced Northrop N-1M was taken in 1943 at Rosamond Dry Lake, California. He is seen discussing events with test pilot Moye Stephens. Of interest is the Lockheed Orion 9C Special, at that time owned by renowned aviator and entrepreneur Paul Mantz, probably involved in air-to-air photography and filming of the N-1M. The Orion configuration shown is as it was raced in the last pre-war Bendix Trophy Race in 1939. While some may not realize it, the Lockheed Orion (and Air Express, Sirius, and Altair) were all based on JKN's 1920's Vega wooden fuselage and wing designs. The Orion 9C Special was unique in that it had an all-metal monocoque fuselage fabricated by the related Detroit Aircraft Corp. The wing and empennage were the typical Burbank wooden products. Mr. Northrop was a gracious, unassuming man , ever willing to be helpful. He lived modestly in the Pacific Palisades suburb of Los Angeles. *Roy Wolford via Gerald Balzer*

It must have been a marvelous day for neophyte naval aviators at NAS Pensacola when the USN began to replace ancient Vought O3U-3s for advanced seaplane work, such as catapulting and rough water operations. Although the BuAer purchased far more Curtiss SO3C Seamews in various models, it is to somebody's credit that the cadets did not have to use them in training. None went to places like Pensacola or Corpus Christi to the best of our knowledge. While there were Timm N2T-1s, Vultee SNV-1s and even Curtiss-Wright SNC-1s, cadets did not have to fly the bedeviled Seamews. On the other hand, we know that Vought Kingfishers were still used by naval reserve squadrons for some time after Japan surrendered and combat passed into history. *USN via R. Starinchak*

173

As it was before self-service. One of Donald Douglas's DB-7B Boston III intruder bombers (or perhaps this was one built by Boeing in Seattle for a total of 781 of that specific model) is shown upon arrival at New York's Floyd Bennett Field, sometime in 1941. These derivatives of the Northrop-designed, Douglas El Segundo-built Model 7B – as redesigned and initially built in Santa Monica – turned out to be most useful for low-level assaults on ground targets where speed was a necessity. They served the RAF well in several categories, and in the variety of Douglas A-20 models they performed meritoriously through the entire length of WWII, including in Russia.   *Howard Levy*

174

Goodyear Aircraft Co., producer of virtually all light-than-aircraft (LTA) airships in the United States was, in 1941, manufacturing LTAs at a very slow rate for the USN. There was essentially no market elsewhere in the world. Without building a new plant, Goodyear was able to move quickly into sub-assembly manufacturing – when recruited under OPM inducements – at Akron, Ohio, within the spacious dirigible building in which the *Akron* and *Macon* were erected in the 1930s. Where necessary, OPM was empowered to obtain necessary critical machine tools from companies not involved in National Defense programs. This parking lot scene, filmed in December 1941, was repeated with monotonous regularity throughout America until Japan capitulated in 1945. No new cars appeared in such scenes throughout the war. *Office of War Information*

LEFT The scene is set in late 1940 according to the spry, active photographer some sixty years later. Big-wheel passenger locomotives of the period, like this "Chicago Limited," was pictured at East Orange, N.J., as it pounded the rails in the direction of Illinois. Steam engines, in those days, dominated the railroads but diesel-powered streamliners were coming on strong. The railroads carried the bulk of all freight, troops, armaments and civilian passengers across, up and down the entire United States and Canada. It was a period when President Roosevelt pledged guns, tanks, ships and aircraft – not to mention all-important food and oil – to aid Great Britain is it faced the Nazis alone. The Neutrality Patrol was established to protect shipping from German submarine attacks off our Eastern shores. A random collection of obsolete to first-line aircraft, ranging from Grumman F2F-1 fighters and Vought SBU-1 scouts flying as dive-bombers to Consolidated P2Y flying boats, patrolled the waters offshore, committed to attacking U-boats even beyond the normal legal limits. The railroads mustered every piece of rolling stock in the nation to move coal, iron, oil, gasoline, anything and everything. If it could move, it was to be repaired, restored, refurbished to assist in carrying the load. War? Americans not close to our Eastern shoreline were more interested in the battles raging in the new film, "Gone with the Wind," than they were in combat in North Africa or Russia. Middle America seemed unaware of the terrible loss of life and ships still within sight of shore dwellers from Maine to Florida. But the railroad trains moved as never before. *E. W. Simpson*

RIGHT Of course Hawaii is a different world, and why shouldn't its railroad cars and engines scaled accordingly. Logically, the cars are scaled to the passengers, but anything goes in the horsepower department. Those railway cars are not cloaked in camouflage paint; that is their normal peacetime color coat, aimed at attracting customers. (?) Perhaps the engine is pushing to keep the dirty smoke out of the passengers' lungs considering that the open windows signify no air-conditioning. A person might win a bet that the "donkey" engine and drab passenger cars predated the turn of the century. In early post-Japanese attack days when the island was bulging with sailors, soldiers, marines and AAF personnel, the Oahu Railway was a real novelty attraction. *E. W. Simpson, Jr.*

Sikorsky had been a major manufacturer of water-based aircraft in 1940 for more than a decade. His commercial S-40 and S-42 flying boats (one version of the S-40 was amphibious) had been pioneers in over water pioneering flights with Pan Am. The builder's S-43 commercial amphibian was used in many venues all over the world. BuAer had procured several of the twin-engine amphibians under the naval designation JRS-1, used primarily by utility squadrons such as VJ-4 as indicated on this JRS-1. Some of these airplanes were fitted with bomb racks to carry depth charges when they flew on Neutrality Patrol duty to combat German U-boats. They were apparently satisfactory in service as target-tow aircraft. Naval aviation could not survive without good utility airplanes. It appears that proper GSE (ground support equipment) was in short supply. No sailor should ever have been compelled to stand on the very top of any stepladder, especially one that was probably 12 feet high. But, we are looking back sixty years and the world has changed. BuAer/Starinchak

RIGHT and OPPOSITE While the unloved 1939 wedding of Vought Aircraft and Sikorsky Aviation was still almost a honeymoon, the Vought V-166B design received the blessing of the USN BuAer, resulting in an order for a single XF4U-1 prototype on 11 June 1938, to be powered by the experimental Navy-sponsored Pratt & Whitney XR-2800-2 engine. In those recession days, fifteen months before war erupted in Europe, there was no urgency for design and fabrication. Therefore, the prototype, with an XR-2800-4 engine, did not make its first flight until 29 May 1940, a bit over sixteen months after the Army Air Corps Lockheed XP-38 was first flown. That XP-38 attained a speed of more than 400 mph in February 1939, long before the XF4U-1 was said to be the first American fighter to exceed that figure. (The distorted facts about that XF4U-1 "record" have been perpetuated in various books to this day.) United Aircraft Corporation, probably under pressure from the government, dissolved the wedding of Vought and Sikorsky in 1942. In the meantime, the initial production F4U-1 Corsair, BuNo. 02153, took off for the first time on 25 June 1942. Less than one *week* later, no less than two dozen (24) combat ready Lockheed P-38F Lightnings in five elements led by five Boeing B-17Es of the mass formation were on the first phase of Operation BOLERO. That phase included 49 Flying Fortresses, 52 Douglas C-47s and 80 Lightnings to be the first combat aircraft in history to fly across the vast North Atlantic Ocean. And it was being done by formations, not a single aircraft. For its part, the Vought F4U-1 was the predecessor of thousands of Corsairs to achieve the distinction of being top and longest lasting naval fighter aircraft of at least the first half century. And more. The two photos show test pilot Boone T. Guyton with that first production Corsair at the Stratford, Connecticut, airfield from which that fighter was flown. *UAC/Author*

178

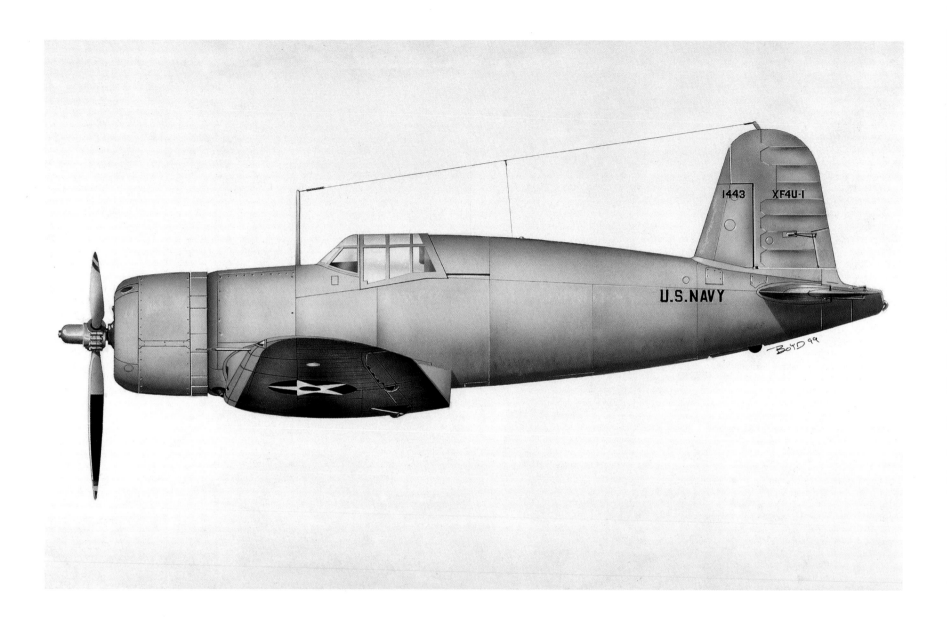

Chance Vought Aircraft's design model V-166B was chosen to be the BuAer's XF4U-1 navy shipboard fighter in 1938 and a contract was awarded on June 11. Powered by a new experimental Pratt & Whitney XR-2800-4 radial engine, the prototype Corsair first flew on 29 May 1940 with test pilot Lyman A. Bullard at the controls, flying out of Bridgeport Municipal Airport, Stratford, Conn., for 38 minutes.

Future RSOs (rear seat occupants) are seen receiving instruction on the finer points of defensive gunnery from an experienced Chief Gunnery Mate and an officer, most likely at NAS Miami (Florida) in 1940-41. The training aircraft is actually an obsolescent, probably obsolete, Curtiss SBC-3 or –4 dive bomber only (then) recently withdrawn from first-line service aboard an aircraft carrier. Had it not been for the advent of the Douglas SBD Dauntless dive bombers at just the right time, our brave crews might well have been thrown into combat episodes in other Curtiss Helldivers like this one and equally slow and obsolete Northrop BT-1 dive bombers, predecessors of the Douglas SBD series. In first-line service, would the BT-1s have been named Doubtful or Dubious? Numerous Curtiss SBCs were turned over to the French for their *Aeronavale* either on land or aboard the carrier *Bearn,* but with the capitulation of France in June 1940, their fate was sealed. They rotted away at the island of Martinique.   *Courtesy R. Starinchak*

Both a National Guard North American O-47B and an Army Air Corps Vultee BT-13 (early series), resplendent in their pre-war colorful paint schemes, were photographed at a naval air station in Florida in the early months of 1941. Vultee's "Vibrators" – their most commonly used identifier – went into mass production for basic training in 1940 and remained in production well into 1944. They were simple aircraft and ruggedly built at a reasonable price. The prototype Model 54 seemed to be right on target for the job from the beginning, and they were very producible. Gerard "Gerry" Vultee's BT-13 and BT-15 twins (Navy SNV-1) contributed tremendously to the war effort. On the other hand, North American's fine O-47 observation airplanes were hardly a factor in WWII, unless you count their contributions to the pre-Pearl Harbor war games significant in a minor way. That was not North American Aviation's fault; the entire blame had to be placed at the feet of the War Department's hierarchy, especially those who refused to believe in aviation as a major player. Gen. Billy Mitchell had it all right from the beginning. Perhaps it was his flamboyant style – he did have more than average ego – that made him intolerable to old-line Army and Navy authorities. *E. W. Simpson, Jr.*

As a North American BT-9 rests in the sun, a Douglas DC-3 airliner can be seen on landing final approach in 1941. The British RAF version of this trainer was known as the Yale, while our USN version was designated NJ-1. (In Navy parlance, the letter N stood for trainer and the J stood for North American Aviation.) Strangely, the S in a later SNJ series stood for scout, a fact probably unknown to the majority of those who flew them. *E. W. Simpson, Jr.*

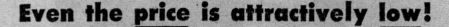

In December 1941, before the Pearl Harbor attack and debacle, generally speaking it was quite normal for 1942 American car models to be in the marketplace. In those days, foreign cars were visible only in New York or California. They were rarities. Changeover time for the industry, mostly centered in Michigan, was generally arranged in the month of October. Plants were normally expected to shut down, especially for major model changes other than facelifts, for about three weeks for tooling and inventory changes. This ad appearing in the December 8, 1941, issue of the venerable Detroit Free Press, then published for 111 years, depicts the newest model of the 1942 Packard Clipper, a so-called fastback model. While that $1283 price seems to be awesomely low, it is appropriate to point out that a new Cadillac 62 fastback coupe had a price tag in the low $1400 range. This author/publisher, barely out of high school and employed in the burgeoning defense industry as America came out of years of Depression and Recession, was able to purchase a new Ford V-8 convertible for a full price of $1077 just three short months after my eighteenth birthday (with absolutely no financial help from any person). In fact, in retrospect I should have purchased the 1941 Mercury, a better-looking car for just $100 more. The Great Depression had taught us to be very conservative. Incredibly, one month later I drove over the Ambassador Bridge to Windsor, Ontario, Canada and tried to enlist for flight training in the RCAF. (It had to be madness.) Rejected for vision problems, I retreated to Detroit and my job. Youthful impatience was hobbled, thanks to an alert flight surgeon. However, it was obvious that I was not going to fly Spitfires in England. Of course December 7 was still one month away. It is well to notice that after more than a century of publication, a daily newspaper was still priced at three cents, the price of a first-class postage stamp. Automobile production for civilian sales was soon to come to an abrupt halt. *Warren Bodie Collection*

When the December 8, 1941, EXTRA edition of the Detroit Free Press was printed in the wee hours of the morning, it must have become the most astonishing headline on that newspaper in its 111-year existence. Of course the other city newspapers – the Detroit Times and the Detroit News had equally expressive headlines. A Honolulu, Hawaii, newspaper, the Honolulu Advertiser illustrated here carried a very disturbing headline exactly a week earlier that warned of an impending attack by the Japanese. Evidently official proclamations issued by America's State Department went unheeded by our own military and naval force commanders. The headlines are authentic, with no sign of "cut-and-paste" activity discerned on close examination. (There were no PC or Macintosh computers in those days.) Therefore, on Sunday December 7, the Japanese Navy struck Hawaii with a near fatal thrust. Only by strokes of luck, not brilliance on the part of our military and naval leaders, did our pitifully puny aircraft carrier force escape disaster, along with our *two* modern battleships. Contact with twentieth century staff members employed by the Advertiser's editorial department even brought forth a denial in that century that such a headline appeared under their masthead. So much for historical interest!   *Warren Bodie Coll.*

Hellfire and Valhalla face the valiant. Appearing in what may we be the one and only honest-to-goodness 35mm Kodachrome view surviving from the disaster at Pearl Harbor are acts of heroism beyond comprehension. Five sailors in a motor launch are seen deliberately dashing headlong into maelstrom on that unforgettable day, December 7, 1941. Firmly established by analysis, this shows the USS *West Virginia* (BB48), one of our most powerful battleships of the so-called "Big Five" that survived the 1920s Washington Naval Treaty. It was a graceful, Clipper-bowed, well-armed battleship mounting nine 16-inch/45-caliber guns. However, with a standard "treaty" displacement of only 31,800 tons and just 27,300 horsepower driving her, she was essentially a World War I weapon. Concurrently, the first of six of our 2-Ocean Fleet battleships, the USS *North Carolina* (BB55), displaced 35,000 tons and was urged along by 115,000 horsepower. The target of several bombs and at least nine torpedoes, the *West Virginia* was that day sitting on the bottom in forty feet of water of East Loch in Pearl Harbor. It was also listing to port about ten degrees, while the entire bow aft to the foremast, was surrounded by burning oil. The *West Virginia* and her partner USS *Tennessee* (BB43) are identifiable by their cage masts rather than tripod masts because planned modernizations had been delayed to allow concentrated effort on new battlewagons. In this photograph *Tennessee* may be seen hull down in mud with water at deck level. Two sailors can be seen standing on a lower platform of the *West Virginia's* foremast with flames below their perch. The launch is headed toward men spotted in the water near the battleship's hull. At that moment, the USS *Arizona* (BB39) had already blown up aft of the *Tennessee*, her superstructure and hull torn apart by a bomb hit on the No. 2 turret magazine. That there were any survivors from the massive explosions is itself a miracle. This is indeed a historical photograph, only seen previously in black and white image in LIFE'S PICTORIAL HISTORY OF WORLD WAR II, published in 1950. These two warships survived to fight another day despite their serious wounds, thanks to America's Arsenal of Democracy. When they did return to fight, they were extensively modernized with far greater ability to compete with the IJN's more modern, treaty-violating ships. Lest we forget, the Japanese never apologized for this and other international law violations.

JAPS-U.S. AT WAR screams the EXTRA edition of The Detroit Free Press on Monday, December 8, 1941. HAWAII AND MANILA BOMBED was printed in a normal headline font. Here was a 111-year-old newspaper with a staff probably shaken as never before by the news. Obviously, every other newspaper in the country, except possibly the Daily Worker, was literally screaming the alarm at every American who could read. But what was it like for most Americans on Sunday morning not long before noon in the Eastern U.S. Or any place in the nation at that time. Well, I can tell you first hand what it was like to a young defense plant worker, just six months out of high school. I recall those days as if it was last week. It was daylight on Sunday morning when I arrived home from the plant in my brand new Ford V8 convertible. Yes, a new car in 1941, literally only months out of that extension of the Great Depression, referred to as the Roosevelt Recession. On the day of my eighteenth birthday I had landed this remarkable job and was soon working six days a week on the midnight shift. Bearings were like the heart of machinery, and that is what we were making. Briefly, I sat in an ultra comfortable chair and slipped into the arms of Morpheus in seconds. Awakened by my mother at sometime around 1000 hours, I turned on our No Stoop, No Sqaut, No Squint Philco console radio. Within seconds I heard the words about the Japanese attack on Honolulu and Pearl Harbor. Strangely, to some, this was not a surprise to me. All male members of my family, clear back to the Civil War, had been military people in one form or another. As a history buff on aviation, I was well aware of what was going on in recent years in Spain and China and South American countries. To me, Prime Minister Chamberlain of England had been totally duped by Hitler. The P.M. was a true non-violent type, not a realist. Of course I blamed FDR for letting this sneak attack happen, but soon realized that without his aviation and naval buildup in the 1930s, we would have taken a far greater punishment. In politics, I would be considered non-partisan. Principles are more important than party or politician. So, that was the beginning of my December 7, just a month after I had tried to enlist in the RCAF for pilot training, across the Detroit River in Windsor, Canada. Right eye vision of 20/400 was the cruel, constantly repetitive phrasing I had become accustomed to hearing for months. For the next sixty days, I worked seven nights a week on midnight shift, then headed for the aircraft industry in California. A piece of the history pie. *Warren Bodie Files*

188

Glossary

AAS	Army Air Service
AAC	Army Air Corps
AAF	Army Air Forces, also Army Air Field
ACS	Army Chief of Staff
ATC	Air Transport Command
AVG	American Volunteer Group (Flying Tigers)
BHP	Brake horsepower
B/J	Berliner-Joyce Aircraft Corp.
BOLERO (Operation)	Transatlantic delivery of USAAF aircraft by air
BOLERO	Buildup of USAAF airpower in the U.K. to attack Fortress Europe
BuAer	USN Bureau of Aeronautics
B-V-D	Boeing-Vega-Douglas group created to produce B-17 Flying Fortresses
CG	Commanding General
CO	Commanding Officer
ETO	European Theater of Operations
FAA	British Fleet Air Arm (Royal Navy)
FAD	Fairfield Air Depot
GHQ AF	General Headquarters Air Force (Combat Command, USAAC)
IAS	Indicated Air Speed
L.A.T.	Lockheed Air Terminal, Burbank, Calif.
Mach's No./Mach No.	Dr. Mach's No. (relative airspeed to speed of sound)
MD	Materiel Division
MoS	Ministry of Supply (England)
MTO	Mediterranean Theater of Operations
NAA	North American Aviation

NACA	National Advisory Committee for Aeronautics
NAF	Naval Aircraft Factory
NAS	Naval Air Station
NRA	National Recovery Act (under Roosevelt administration)
ONI	Office of Naval Intelligence
OPM	Office of Production Management
RAE	Royal Aeronautical Establishment
SWPA	Southwest Pacific Area
TAS	True airspeed
T.H.	Territory of Hawaii
TIAS	True indicated airspeed
USCG	U.S. Coast Guard
USMC	U.S. Marine Corps
USN	U.S. Navy
USAAC	U.S. Army Air Corps
USAAF	U.S. Army Air Forces
VB	Naval Bomber Squadron
VF	Naval Fighter Squadron
VJ	Naval Utility Squadron
VO	Naval Observation Squadron
VP	Naval Patrol Squadron
VS	Naval Scout Squadron
VT	Naval Torpedo Squadron
WEP	War Emergency Power
WPA	Works Progress Administration
WPB	War Production Board
ZI	Zone of the Interior

Index

PHOTOGRAPHS and CAPTIONS

**Nakajima A2N2
(Type 90-II)**

Mitsubishi A5M2 - otsu